CROCHET LACE

INNOVATIONS

This book is dedicated to all the teachers in my life and to three in particular: Mom, whose love for me taught me to love myself; Dad and Lorraine Lerro, my other mom, who both taught me we should cherish our loved ones while they are here.

CROCHET LACE

INNOVATIONS

20 Dazzling Designs

IN BROOMSTICK, HAIRPIN, TUNISIAN, AND EXPLODED LACE

DORIS CHAN

POTTER
CRAFT

NEW YORK

CONTENTS

INTRODUCTION

I AM WILLING TO WAGER THAT MOST AMERICANS HAVE SOMETHING CROCHETED IN THEIR POSSESSION WHETHER THEY'RE AWARE OF IT OR NOT—AN AFGHAN MADE BY MOM, A VINTAGE DOILY PASSED DOWN FROM A GREAT-AUNT, CLOTHING OFF THE RACK FROM A DEPARTMENT STORE. Millions of people are right this minute creating crochet in the only way possible—through the work of millions of pairs of hands, painstakingly inserting hooks into billions of stitches. For the most part, the work of those millions of hands remains largely unsung and underappreciated because, traditionally, crochet has been considered a home art, practiced mainly by homemakers (women) in solitude. Everybody knows someone who crochets or used to do it. I hear that all the time. Cool or uncool, fashionable or not, crochet is just what we do. Quietly.

Something amazing happens when we take crochet out of the home and into the wider world. Say you're sitting in the customer lounge of the auto service department wearing your favorite crocheted sweater or shawl because, dang, it gets cold hanging around next to a service bay. Other customers with reading materials or young children are already signaling that they are occupied and would not welcome any intrusion, including the bad news from the repair guy. But, like Felix the Cat with his bag of tricks, you pull your current work in progress out of your bag and make magic happen. With your delicious yarn and flying fingers, you become an attention magnet and the target for an inevitable barrage of comments: "What are you knitting? "Did you knit that?" And "Gee, my grandmother knits all the time."

Please accept your role as crochet model/spokesperson/ambassador graciously. Recognize these as teachable moments. By patiently explaining that you are crocheting, that knitting is done with two pointed sticks while crochet is done with a hook, you are teaching that person something she, or more likely he, did not know. By showing off the beautiful work of your hands you are generating interest and curiosity and maybe, just maybe, you have planted the seed of desire in others to learn how to do that, too. This means that we millions of crocheters are all potential teachers.

"Crochet is everywhere."

My mother was my first crochet teacher. Although Mom does not read patterns, she has always understood my unquenchable thirst for printed crochet and craft materials, because she searched them out everywhere she went. She grabbed anything with pictures of stuff made from yarn to put in my eager hands, even when she had no idea what was inside.

That's how I met Broomstick lace. One day a few years ago, my mom presented me with a stack of old booklets she'd scored at a flea market. One, in particular, caused my heart to jump. It was called *Exciting Jiffy-Lace*, a circa-1970 collection of designs using Broomstick technique. The clothes were dated but the fabric I saw in those photos was fascinating, with rows of impossibly lacy swirls that reminded me of the "eyes" of a peacock tail feather. Upon realizing that I'd need a stick (a giant knitting needle) and a protracted period of practice in order to make this fabric, I sort of gave up on it. I tried re-creating the same look using regular crochet, but it wasn't easy, and the results were far from satisfactory.

Not long afterward, inside a goodie bag from a yarn event, I received a set of "speed sticks," short, thick knitting needles intended for making quick scarves. Since I no longer knit, I almost gave them away to any other attendee who would take them, but thought better of it and stashed the sticks with so many other abandoned knitting tools I had at home. By coincidence, one happy day both the Jiffy-Lace booklet and the speed sticks were in my hands at the same time, and after a couple of attempts, I had made Broomstick lace my own.

My first introductions to other old techniques did not go so well. Many years ago, I inherited a bag of knitting and crochet tools from a friend's attic. It was like Christmas. Included in the bounty was a funny kind of loom. On the back of the original packaging there were very basic instructions on how to make Hairpin strips. So what the heck, I tried playing with this new toy. Ready to tackle a pattern for a gorgeous stole I saw in a '50s-era magazine, I balked at the first line, which called for a strip containing over five hundred loops using a fine fingering-weight yarn. I struggled for days and wound up with a horrible tangled mess that got stashed with the loom in some deservedly dark corner.

In that same bag of toys were several tools that were crochet hooks on one end and long knitting needles on the other end. My 1971 edition of the *Good Housekeeping Complete Book of Needlecraft* told me these were Afghan (Tunisian) hooks. The only projects this volume offered in this technique were thick, heavy solid things; a "soaker" (a baby's diaper cover, I assumed) and a "slipon" sweater that was completely covered with cross-stitched and embroidered embellishments, nothing I considered worth the effort. Those hooks were also banished to the corner.

Obviously, there's only so far you can take yourself. I am not, by nature, a joiner. Also, having plodded through stultifying years of higher education, I vowed never to set foot in a classroom again. So here's the irony: Becoming a member of the Crochet Guild of America, attending CGOA conferences over the past five years, and diving into everything from Professional Development Day to classes to fashion shows, and, along the way amassing a network of the dearest crochet comrades, were the best things I ever did for my craft. Sitting and learning from an instructor whose work you admire and whose skills you covet is the way to take your own crochet to a new level.

In fact, I gained such skills that I now consider it to have been worth dragging my sorry butt to classes at 8 or 9 a.m., thanks to the teachers who come to the events and offer their best. From Nancy Nehring's "Designing for Larger Sizes," to Darla Fanton's "Introduction to Tunisian Crochet," to Jennifer Hansen's "Stylish Introduction to Hairpin Lace," session by session, practice swatch by practice swatch, I was expanding my crochet comfort zone to include some of the techniques I once dismissed, and now dare to incorporate in my designs.

At the time this book is being born, I have yet to formally or professionally teach crochet. I thought you had to be an expert before you presented yourself as an instructor, and I may be many things, a fiberazza, a tinkerer, a crochet advocate, a space cadet, a prime suspect, but I am no expert.

But here's the thing. The optimal time to teach is when you yourself have just absorbed something so fantastic, are so totally fired up with the process that you simply can't wait to share it with someone. Great teaching isn't about parading your expertise; it's about bringing someone else to your skill level along the path where you've just been.

Why would you want to learn any of this old stuff? I admit that I once prejudged Broomstick, Hairpin, and Tunisian crochet as prissy or stodgy, antiquated methods, and for years ignored the possibilities. Why mess with this "pseudo" crochet and fumble around with a gang of unfamiliar tools when I was having so much fun with regular crochet? The short answer is because it looks so cool and so unlike anything you can do with regular crochet.

In this book are the fruits of the lessons I learned—garments and accessories that put time-honored techniques in a more modern light. In wandering through this book, you may encounter ways of crocheting that are unfamiliar to you. Or you may find reasons to reacquaint yourself with beloved techniques you already know: Broomstick, Hairpin, Tunisian, motifs, lace, a smattering of beading. While I'll never stop being a student of crochet, and can never claim to be an expert in any of these techniques, I know it is my responsibility and my pleasure to pass on what I have recently learned. Whether you approach this book as a guide into unknown crochet territory, as a source for engaging projects that may inspire you to revisit languishing skills, or as yet another "Doris Does Lace" manual, I hope you'll be reading between the lines. Because written in here is all the excitement and wonder I felt while discovering this stuff for myself. And if you achieve one, just one "a-ha!" moment, then I will have done my job.

How to Use This Book

There are many benefits to incorporating lace into your crocheted wearables. Open, lacy stitches help keep your crochet lightweight and airy. And beautiful lace will invariably catch the eye of the beholder and hold center stage, keeping the attention away from the places where you'd rather not have attention paid. Think of a how a lacy collar on a jacket draws the eye to a pretty neck and face; how the lace border on a skirt shows off shapely legs and takes the spotlight away from the hips; how a lace belt emphasizes a curvy waist.

I've loaded the first three chapters with new ways to make lace with the alternative crochet techniques, Broomstick, Hairpin, and Tunisian, respectively. Please study the tutorials for each chapter if you are a newbie, and do a bit of practice before jumping into the designs that follow.

The next three chapters continue my obsession with exploded or relaxed-gauge regular crochet, my favorite way to roll. By loosening up crocheted fabric using larger hooks and lacy stitches, you can achieve the lightness and supple drape that make modern crochet garments so wearable.

The last chapter is a deeper exploration of two specific garment designs, employing a patterning convention that saves space and gives the crocheter the most options. It presents the two templates, Jacket 101 and Skirt 101, that are quoted throughout the other chapters. By using the basic garment templates and making the alterations and shaping options that are best for your body, you'll be able to get a great fit.

All the projects in this book are doable by crocheters with basic skills, the ability to read and understand written patterns and diagrams, a dash of confidence, and a bit of faith. I have tried to follow the skill levels as outlined in the "Yarn Standards and Guidelines" handbook developed by the Craft Yarn Council of America. Please visit www.yarnstandards.com to view and download this useful publication.

Please read each pattern all the way through before beginning to crochet. For a number of the garments, the pattern requires you to bounce back and forth between the Chapter 7 templates, the stitch pattern notes, and the instructions for your size in each particular design. I regret any confusion and cursing that ensues, but once you mark out each step you need to take, all should be clear.

Please feel free to make yarn substitutions. Use any yarns that will work to the stated gauge and result in the fabric you want.

And if you are not yet familiar with the chainless foundation stitch, the foundation single crochet (Fsc), please see the section in the Resources beginning on page 134 to learn it. When I first began writing this foundation into my patterns, it had no generally accepted name, so I called it base ch/sc. But the stitch has since been standardized and is now known as Fsc.

Once you have a solid grasp of the techniques, you'll be ready to unleash your own creativity and add that *je ne sais quoi*, a touch of lace, to your crochet.

SKILL LEVELS FOR CROCHET

◆ ◆ ◆ ◆	BEGINNER	Projects for first-time crocheters using basic stitches. Minimal shaping.
◆ ◆ ◆ ◆	EASY	Projects using yarn with basic stitches, repetitive stitch patterns, simple color changes, and simple shaping and finishing.
◆ ◆ ◆ ◆	INTERMEDIATE	Projects using a variety of techniques, such as basic lace patterns or color patterns, mid-level shaping and finishing
◆ ◆ ◆ ◆	EXPERIENCED	Projects with intricate stitch patterns, techniques and dimension, such as non-repeating patterns, multi-color techniques, fine threads, small hooks, detailed shaping and refined finishing.

Broomstick Lace

One Hook, One Big Stick

BROOMSTICK CROCHET IS ALSO KNOWN AS "JIFFY-LACE" AND by the wonderfully descriptive names "peacock's eye" or "bird's eye" crochet. It makes the loveliest, laciest fabric imaginable without too much fuss. The concept is simple: You pull up extremely tall loops from a row of regular crochet and hold them open, then gather chunks of loops into swirly "eyes" using regular crochet stitches.

It is possible to make similar lace without the use of a second tool (see the "new" *Harmony Guides Basic Crochet Stitches*, "Broomstick Lace," page 173), but it requires an experienced hand to keep all the loops uniform. More commonly, you'll find this technique made with the aid of a "broomstick" (once the actual handle of a broom), also called a pin or a mandrel, a cylindrical rod that has a pointed end for ease of slipping on loops, and perhaps a knob or stop at the other end. Today there is a perfect tool for this task, widely available at any craft or yarn shop or site, a jumbo knitting needle—size 17 (12.75mm), size 19 (15mm), size 35 (19mm), and the big-as-a-horse-leg size 50 (25mm); all make useful sticks.

Broomstick lace itself does not offer many variations on the basic theme. However, rows of Broomstick can easily be integrated into any fabric of regular stitches, so it is a neat way to add openness, texture, and interest to your crochet.

BROOMSTICK TUTORIAL

Broomstick crochet uses a second tool to load and hold all the loops in a row (loop row), to be worked off in the following row with normal crochet stitches (crochet row). Generally, the bigger the stick, the taller the loops, the lacier the fabric. For the designs here, you will use the following guidelines where the stick is always to your left and your crochet hook is employed as you would normally. The work is never turned, so the right side is always facing. Loops may be pulled up through the front loop, through the back loop, or through both loops of a crochet stitch, according to the specific pattern instructions. Although the loops are slipped onto the stick without twisting, interestingly, due to the nature and direction of the crochet yarn over, my preferred technique gives each loop an automatic twist, like making a back loop, which I find particularly attractive.

MAKING BROOMSTICK FABRIC

Make the foundation (Fsc) as directed, then turn the foundation so the loop on the hook is to the left and the row of single crochet runs along the top. You will now be moving "backwards" on the work, from left to right, pulling up and loading loops onto the stick.

FIRST LOOP ROW

1. Slip the loop from the hook onto the stick without twisting (a).

2. Unless otherwise directed, skip the first sc. *Insert hook through the back loop only of the next sc (b).

3. YO and draw up a long loop, slip loop onto the stick (c).

Repeat from * for length of the foundation.

FIRST CROCHET ROW

4. Insert (now-empty) hook under the first group of loops as directed in the pattern, let's say five. You do not want to twist the loops here, so slip the hook into the loops the same way as they are seated on the stick.

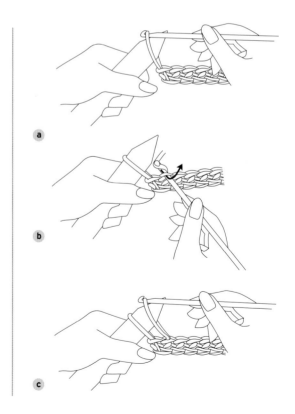

5. Holding all 5 loops together as one, slide them off the stick (5 loops now on the hook). Bring the feeder yarn loosely up the back of the work to the hook, YO, and draw a loop through all 5 loops on the hook (one loop on hook) (d).

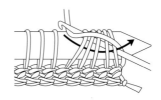

6. YO and ch 1 to lock the edge (e).

7. Insert hook through the center of the same five loops (f).

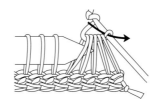

8. Make 5 sc in the group (g).

*Insert hook in the next 5 loops on the stick, slide this group off the stick, make 5 sc through all 5 loops. Repeat from * to the end of the row. Without turning and without twisting, slip the loop remaining on hook onto the stick.

SECOND LOOP ROW

Skip the first sc, pull up a loop through the back loop only in each sc across.

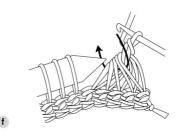

SECOND CROCHET ROW

Same as the first crochet row.

For pattern, work [second loop row, second crochet row] as required.

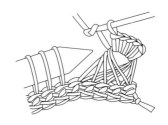

tips for success

Generally, you will make the same number of stitches into each group as there are loops. The exception is when you are shaping the Broomstick fabric with increases and decreases. See individual patterns for instructions on how to do this.

The beginning of the crochet row needs a locking stitch, basically a slip stitch through the group of loops, which carries the feeder yarn from the base of the last loop up to the correct place for crocheting. Keep the locking stitch fairly loose to avoid choking up this edge. The rest of the stitches across the crochet row are normal. Hold onto each group as you work it to avoid distorting the loops. Some crocheters advise you to pull the stick completely out of the loop row before beginning the crochet row. If I do that, I find it impossible to keep all the loops seated in the same direction. Therefore, my preferred method is to work each group of rows off the stick each time.

It may take some practice juggling the hook, stick, and yarn until you figure out for yourself the most efficient and comfortable way to manage everything. I sometimes prop the stick on my lap or against the table where I am working.

The aim is to make your loops neat and even, but not too tight. You have to be able to slide the loops fairly easily up and down the stick.

For very long rows and larger garments, you may need more room than one stick affords. There are a couple of ways to manage long rows. Knitting needles come in pairs (how nice is that!) so you can pull half the loops with one, half with the other. If you wish, you can use a supersized circular knitting needle with a flexible cable.

If, for some reason, you only have one of the correct size stick, pull up as many as will fit, then either (1) drop them off the stick if you can deal with the loops twisting around occasionally, or (2) slip them onto anything handy that will hold them, like any other long knitting needle or cable, or even a long marker yarn. Then continue pulling loops with your one stick. In the same ways, you can manage Broomstick loops around a small opening like an armhole or sleeve, putting half the loops on one stick or holder, half the loops on another.

SOOLIN BELT

TURN A LONG STRIP OF BROOMSTICK LACE INTO A BELT WITH THE ADDITION OF SOME HARDWARE AT ONE END. CHOOSE YARN THAT IS STURDY AND HAS SOME BODY, LIKE COTTON, FIRMLY TWISTED WOOL, LINEN, HEMP, OR BLENDS CONTAINING THESE FIBERS. THE YARN WEIGHT SHOWN IS DK, BUT FEEL FREE TO USE YOUR CHOICE AND ADJUST THE HOOK ACCORDINGLY, BEGINNING WITH A FOUNDATION AS WIDE AS YOU WANT YOUR BELT TO BE AND WORKING TO THE LENGTH DESIRED.

SKILL LEVEL: EASY ✦ ✦ ✦ ✦

SIZE
2" (5cm) wide, length made to measure, adjustable with D-ring buckle; sample shown is 36" (91cm) long

MATERIALS
Lanaknits Hemp for knitting Allhemp6; 100% long fiber hemp; 3½ oz (100g)/165 yd (150m) 〔4〕

—One hank in #011 Raspberry, enough for any length belt

Size H-8 (5mm) crochet hook

Size G-6 (4mm) crochet hook, for finishing

Size 19 (15mm) knitting needle for stick, the 10" (25.5cm) long "scarf sticks" are perfect for narrow projects like this, but any length needle is fine

Yarn needle

Two 2" (5cm) wide metal D-rings for buckle, or purchased belt hardware

GAUGE (NOT CRITICAL)
In Broomstick lace, using larger hook, 15 sts = 2" (5cm), (loop row, crochet row) 4 times = 4" (10cm)

STITCHES USED
Fsc (see page 134 for technique), sl st, ch, sc

STITCH PATTERN
See Broomstick Tutorial (page 14) for detailed instructions on this technique.

This pattern uses five loops per group, with five single crochet in each group, and starts with a foundation that is a multiple of five stitches minus two.

INSTRUCTIONS
Using the smaller hook to keep the belt end neat, Fsc 13. Turn the foundation so the sc edge is on top, put the last loop on hook onto the stick (counts as one loop), switch to the larger hook.

LP (LOOP) ROW 1 Insert hook tfl of the first sc, draw up a loop and put it on the stick, pull up a loop tbl in each of the next 11 sc, pull up a loop tfl in the last sc, pull up a loop tbl in the same last sc—15 loops.

C (CROCHET) ROW 1 5 sc in each group of 5 loops—15 sc (3 groups of 5 each).

LP ROW 2 Pull up a loop tbl of each sc across—15 loops.

C ROW 2 5 sc in each group of 5 loops across—15 sc.

Repeat (Lp Row 2, C Row 2) 33 times or to length desired, work Lp Row 2 once more, switch to the smaller hook, work C Row 2 once more. Fasten off leaving a long tail for assembly. Hold 2 D-rings together with the straight side of the rings against the last row of sc. Thread the ending tail onto the yarn needle, whipstitch densely and firmly, going around the D-rings and through the top loops of the sc row, fasten off. Weave in ends.

STITCH KEY

⋈ = foundation sc (fsc)

⌒ = worked through back loop (tbl)

⌣ = worked through front loop (tfl)

⬭ = chain (ch)

X = single crochet (sc)

= group of broomstick lace loops (5 loops shown)

INARA SCARF

•• ✦ ••

EVERYONE HAS SOME SPECIAL YARNS STASHED AWAY, BITS OF GORGEOUS STUFF IN SMALL
AMOUNTS THAT YOU HAVEN'T YET FIGURED OUT HOW TO USE IN CROCHET. YEARS AGO I
ACQUIRED TWO LITTLE HANKS OF THIS SILK RIBBON, BROUGHT BACK AS A SOUVENIR FROM A
CONFERENCE. BEAUTIFUL AS IT IS, THE RIBBON BECAME A SOURCE OF AGGRAVATION; IT SNAGS
ON AIR. NORMAL CROCHET STITCHES SEEMED TO CRUMPLE, TWIST, AND COMPACT THE RIBBON
TO THE POINT WHERE I WONDERED WHY I BOTHERED. IT WASN'T UNTIL I TRIED BROOMSTICK
LACE THAT I FOUND A TECHNIQUE THAT DOES A SPECTACULAR JOB SHOWING OFF THE BEAUTY OF
RIBBON YARNS. TO SUBSTITUTE A RIBBON THAT'S WIDER THAN ⅛" (3mm), CHOOSE AN APPROPRIATE
LARGER-SIZED CROCHET HOOK AND A THICKER STICK.

SKILL LEVEL: EASY ✦ ✦ ✦ ✦

SIZE
4" (10cm) wide, 50" (127cm) long

MATERIALS
Artyarns Silk Ribbon; 100% Hand
painted silk; 0.88 oz (25g)/128 yd
(118m) (2)

—2 hanks in #111

Size H-8 (5mm) crochet hook

Size 19 (15mm) knitting needle for
stick, the 10" (25.5cm) "scarf sticks" are
perfect for narrow projects like this, but
any length needle is fine

Yarn needle

GAUGE (NOT CRITICAL)
In Broomstick lace, 28 sts = 4" (10cm),
(Loop Row, Crochet Row) 5 times = 4"
(10 cm)

STITCHES USED
Fsc (see page 134 for technique), sl st,
ch, Esc

STITCH DEFINITIONS
Esc (extended single crochet): Insert
hook in the next stitch, YO and draw up
a loop, YO and draw through one loop
on hook, YO and draw through two
loops on hook.

STITCH PATTERN
**See Broomstick Tutorial (page 14) for
detailed instructions on this technique.**

This pattern uses four loops per group,
with four extended single crochet in
each group, and starts with a foundation
that is a multiple of four stitches.

INSTRUCTIONS

Fsc 28, turn the foundation so the sc edge is on top, put the
last loop on hook onto the stick (counts as one loop).

L(OOP) ROW 1 Follow instructions for Tutorial First Loop
Row for 28 loops.

C(ROCHET) ROW 1 4 Esc in each group of 4 loops—28
Esc (7 groups of 4 each).

LP ROW 2 Pull up a loop tbl of each Esc across—28 loops.

C ROW 2 5 Esc in each group of 5 loops across—28 Esc.

Repeat (Lp Row 2, C Row 2) 60 times or to length desired.
Fasten off, weave in ends.

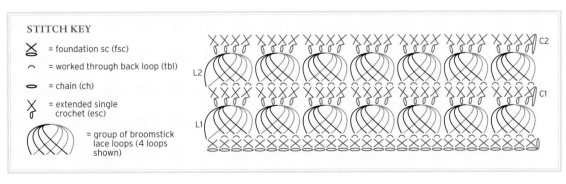

STITCH KEY

⋈ = foundation sc (fsc)

⌒ = worked through back loop (tbl)

⊖ = chain (ch)

✕ = extended single
crochet (esc)

⟨⟨⟨⟨⟩ = group of broomstick
lace loops (4 loops
shown)

MELISANDE VEST

·• ──── •• ✦ •• ──── •·

IF YOU HAVE CROCHETED BROOMSTICK PATTERNS BEFORE, OR IF YOU'VE PRACTICED ENOUGH

AND ARE READY FOR A MORE CHALLENGING PROJECT, HERE IS A SHAPED GARMENT. MELISANDE

OFFERS TECHNIQUES FOR INCREASING BROOMSTICK LACE TO CREATE A SEAMLESS VEST WITH

CAP SLEEVES. THE BUTTONED WAISTBAND GATHERS IN SOME OF THE FULLNESS OF THE BODY FOR

A SLIGHTLY FITTED APPEAL.

THIS GLORIOUS YARN IS WONDERFULLY SOFT WITH SUBTLE COLOR SHADING AND KNITS TO

5½ STITCHES TO THE INCH (2.5cm). FEEL FREE TO SUBSTITUTE ANY MEDIUM SPORTWEIGHT OR

LIGHT DK WEIGHT YARN THAT CAN BE WORKED TO THE CROCHET GAUGE FOR THIS DESIGN.

SKILL LEVEL: EXPERIENCED ✦ ✦ ✦ ✦

SIZE
XS (S, M, L, XL, 2XL); finished bust 33 (36, 40, 43, 45, 48)" (84 [91, 101.5, 109, 112, 122]cm); sample shown is size XS

MATERIALS
Manos Silk Blend; 30% Silk, 70% extrafine wool, kettle dyed; 1.75 oz (50g)/150 yd (135m) (3)

—4 (4, 5, 6, 6, 7) hanks in # 3019 Dove

Size I-9 (5.5mm) crochet hook

Size H-8 (5mm) crochet hook, for armbands if needed to achieve firmer gauge

Size 35 (19mm) knitting needle, for stick; a pair of needles would be nice, but not necessary

Split-ring markers or scraps of yarn for markers

Two buttons, ⅝" (16mm) diameter, as lightweight as possible

Needle and matching thread or self yarn, for sewing buttons

GAUGE
14 Fsc or sc = 4" (10cm)

In Broomstick lace, 4 groups of [4 loops with 4 sc in each group] = 3½" (9cm); 4 times [Loop row, sc row] = 4" (10cm) as crocheted (will block to 4 sets of rows = 4¼" [11cm])

Using I-9 (5.5mm) hook for cluster stitch of waistband, 7 repeats [Cl, ch 1] = 3¾" (9.5cm)

Using H-8 (5mm) hook for cluster stitch of armbands, 8 repeats [Cl, ch 1] = 3½" (9cm)

STITCHES USED
Fsc (see Glossary page 134 for technique), sl st, ch, sc, dc

STITCH DEFINITIONS
CL (SC2TOG CLUSTER) Insert hook in the next ch-1 sp, YO and draw up a loop, insert hook in the top of the next sc cluster, YO and draw up a loop, YO and draw through all 3 loops on hook.

BASIC BROOMSTICK PATTERN
For more about basic Broomstick technique, see Broomstick Tutorial (page 14).

This pattern uses four loops per group, with four single crochet in each group.

—To work even, without increase or decrease, repeat this set for the basic stitch pattern:

LP EVEN Begin with one loop on hook, skip the first sc, pull up a loop tbl in each sc across.

C EVEN 4 sc in each group of 4 loops.

—To increase by one group of 4 at each end of a row, use this Loop row.

LP INC-NECK Begin with one loop on hook, pull up a loop tfl in the first sc, [pull up a loop tbl, pull up a loop tfl] in each of the next 3 sc, work in pattern as established to the last group of 4 sc, [pull up a loop tbl, pull up a loop tfl] in each of the last 4 sc.

—To increase at 4 corners of the yoke, use these rows. A set of Lp/C increases adds 32 loops/8 groups to the yoke. Mark the group at the center of each of 4 corners and move markers up as you go.

LP INC-CORNER Begin with one loop on stick, skip the first sc, *pull up a loop tbl in each sc to the next 8-sc corner, pull up a loop tbl in each of first 2 sc of the corner, [pull up a loop tbl, pull up a loop tfl] in each of the next 4 sc, pull up a loop tbl in each of the last 2 sc of the corner*; repeat from * to * 3 times, pull up a loop tbl in each sc to the end. The 4 loops in the center of each increase become the corner group.

C INC-CORNER *4 sc in each group of 4 loops to the next corner group, 8 sc in the corner group of 4 loops*; repeat from * to * 3 times, 4 sc in each group of 4 loops to the end.

INSTRUCTIONS
Yoke

Fsc 35 (35, 35, 35, 35, 39); turn the foundation so the sc edge is on top and begin work across the sc edge.

Size XS

LP ROW 1 Begin with one loop on stick, skip the first sc, [(pull up a loop tbl, pull up a loop tfl) in the next sc, pull up a loop tbl in the next sc] 17 times—52 loops.

C ROW 1 8 sc in the first group of 4 loops for the corner, 4 sc in the next group of 4 loops, 8 sc in the next group of 4 loops for the corner, [4 sc in the next group of 4 loops] 7 times, 8 sc in the next group of 4 loops for the corner, 4 sc in the next group of 4 loops, 8 sc in the last group of 4 loops for the corner—13 groups; 68 sc.

LP ROW 2 Begin with one loop on hook, skip the first sc, pull up a loop tbl in the next sc, *(pull up a loop tbl, pull up a loop tfl) in each of the next 4 sc of the corner, pull up a loop tbl in each of the remaining 2 sc of the corner, pull up a loop tbl in each sc to the next 8-sc corner, at the corner pull up a loop tbl in each of the next 2 sc*; repeat from * to * 3 times—84 loops.

C ROW 2 Work C Inc-Corner—21 groups; 92 sc.

LP ROW 3 Work Lp Inc-Corner—116 loops.

C ROW 3 Work C Inc-Corner—29 groups; 132 sc.

LP ROW 4 Begin as Lp Inc-Neck; work increases at the corners as Lp Inc-Corner; end as Lp Inc-Neck—156 loops.

C ROW 4 Work C Even—39 groups; 156 sc.

LP ROW 5 Work Lp Even.

C ROW 5 Work C Inc-Corner—39 groups; 172 sc.

LP/C ROWS 6–7 Repeat Lp/C Rows 4–5—196 loops/49 groups; 212 sc.

Size S

LP ROW 1 Begin with one loop on stick, skip the first sc, [pull up a loop tbl in the next sc, (pull up a loop tbl, pull up a loop tfl) in each of the next 3 sc] 8 times, (pull up a loop tbl, pull lp tfl) in the next sc, pull up a loop tbl in the last sc—60 loops.

C ROW 1 8 sc in the first group of 4 loops for the corner, 4 sc in the next group of 4 loops, 8 sc in the next group of 4 loops for the corner, [4 sc in the next group of 4 loops] 9 times, 8 sc in the next group of 4 loops for the corner, 4 sc in the next group of 4 loops, 8 sc in the last group of 4 loops for the corner—15 groups; 76 sc.

LP ROW 2 Begin with one loop on hook, skip the first sc, pull up a loop tbl in the next sc, *(pull up a loop tbl, pull up a loop tfl) in each of the next 4 sc of the corner, pull up a loop tbl in each of the remaining 2 sc of the corner, pull up a loop tbl in each sc to the next 8-sc corner, at the corner pull up a loop tbl in each of the next 2 sc*; repeat from * to * 3 times—92 loops.

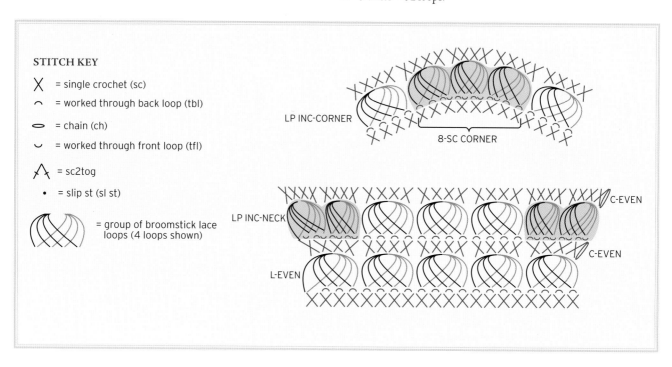

STITCH KEY

X = single crochet (sc)

⌢ = worked through back loop (tbl)

⊖ = chain (ch)

⌣ = worked through front loop (tfl)

⋀ = sc2tog

• = slip st (sl st)

= group of broomstick lace loops (4 loops shown)

LP INC-CORNER

8-SC CORNER

LP INC-NECK

C-EVEN

C-EVEN

L-EVEN

C ROW 2 Work C Inc-Corner—23 groups; 108 sc.

LP ROW 3 Begin as Lp Inc-Neck; work increases at the corners as Lp Inc-Corner; end as Lp Inc-Neck—132 loops.

C ROW 3 Work C Inc-Corner—33 groups; 148 sc.

LP ROW 4 Work Lp Inc-Corner—164 loops.

C ROW 4 Work C Even—41 groups; 164 sc.

LP ROW 5 Begin as Lp Inc-Neck; work Lp Even across; end as Lp Inc-Neck—172 loops.

C ROW 5 Work C Inc-Corner—43 groups; 188 sc.

LP/C ROWS 6–7 Repeat Lp/C Rows 4–5 once—212 loops/53 groups; 228 sc.

Sizes M and L

LP/C ROWS 1–3 S as size S Lp/C Rows 1–3—33 groups; 148 sc.

LP ROW 4 Work Lp Inc-Corner—164 loops.

C ROW 4 Work C Inc-Corner—41 groups; 180 sc.

LP ROW 5 Begin as Lp Inc-Neck; work increases at the corners as Lp Inc-Corner; end as Lp Inc-Neck—204 loops.

C ROW 5 Work C Even—51 groups; 204 sc.

LP ROW 6 Work L Even—204 loops.

C ROW 6 Work C Inc-Corner—51 groups; 220 sc.

LP/C ROWS 7–8 Repeat Lp/C Rows 5–6 once—244 loops/61 groups; 260 sc.

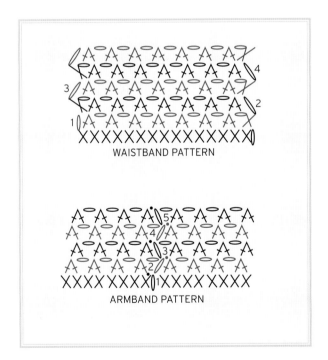

WAISTBAND PATTERN

ARMBAND PATTERN

Size XL

LP/C ROWS 1–2 Same as size S Lp/C Rows 1–2—23 groups; 108 sc.

LP ROW 3 Work Lp Inc-Corner—124 loops.

C ROW 3 Work C Inc-Corner—31 groups; 140 sc.

LP ROW 4 Begin as Lp Inc-Neck; work increases at the corners as Lp Inc-Corner; end as Lp Inc-Neck—164 loops.

C ROW 4 Work C Inc-Corner—41 groups; 180 sc.

LP ROW 5 Work Lp Inc-Corner—196 loops.

C ROW 5 Work C Inc-Corner—49 groups; 212 sc.

LP ROW 6 Begin as Lp Inc-Neck; work increases at the corners as Lp Inc-Corner; end as Lp Inc-Neck—236 loops.

C ROW 6 Work C Even—59 groups; 236 sc.

LP ROW 7 Work Lp Even.

C ROW 7 Work C Inc-Corner—59 groups; 252 sc.

LP/C ROWS 8–9 Repeat Lp/C Rows 6–7 once—276 loops/69 groups; 292 sc.

Size 2XL

LP ROW 1 Begin with one loop on stick, skip the first sc, (pull up a loop tbl, pull up a loop tfl) in each of the next 2 sc, [pull up a loop tbl in the next sc, (pull up a loop tbl, pull up a loop tfl) in each of the next 3 sc] 9 times—68 loops.

C ROW 1 8 sc in the first group of 4 loops for the corner, 4 sc in the next group of 4 loops, 8 sc in the next group of 4 loops for the corner, [4 sc in the next group of 4 loops] 11 times, 8 sc in the next group of 4 loops for the corner, 4 sc in the next group of 4 loops, 8 sc in the last group of 4 loops for the corner—17 groups; 84 sc.

LP/C ROWS 2–3 Same as size S Lp/C Rows 2–3—35 groups; 156 sc.

LP ROW 4 Work Lp Inc-Corner—172 loops.

C ROW 4 Work C Inc-Corner—43 groups; 188 sc.

LP ROW 5 Begin as Lp Inc-Neck; work increases at the corners as Lp Inc-Corner; end as Lp Inc-Neck—212 loops.

C ROW 5 Work C Inc-Corner—53 groups; 228 sc.

LP ROW 6 Work Lp Inc-Corner—244 loops.

C ROW 6 Work C Even—61 groups; 244 sc.

LP ROW 7 Begin as Lp Inc-Neck; work Lp Even across; end as Lp Inc-Neck—252 loops.

C ROW 7 Work C Inc-Corner—63 groups; 268 sc.

LP/C ROWS 8–9 Repeat Lp/ Rows 6–7 once—292 loops/73 groups; 308 sc.

Underarms

Place the last loop of the yoke on hold. There is an 8-sc corner at each of the four corners of the yoke. A section of foundation stitches must be spliced in from corner to corner for each underarm before the fronts and back can be joined as one continuous row for the body.

FIRST UNDERARM With RS facing, join yarn with sl st in the 4th sc of the first front corner, ch 1, Fsc 8 (8, 8, 12, 12, 12), skip to the next 8-sc corner, sl st in 5th sc of the corner, fasten off.

SECOND UNDERARM With RS still facing, join yarn with sl st in the 4th sc of the next corner of the back, ch 1, Fsc 8 (8, 8, 12, 12, 12), skip to the last 8-sc corner, sl st in the 5th sc of the corner, fasten off.

Body

Sizes XS, M, L, and XL begin Row 1 with an increase to complete the front neck shaping; sizes S and 2XL complete the front neck shaping in Row 2.

With RS facing, place the loop on hold onto the stick.

LP ROW 1 According to your size, begin as Lp Inc-Neck (Lp Even, Lp Inc-Neck, Lp Inc-Neck, Lp Inc-Neck, Lp Even), *work as Lp Even until the next 4 sc before the underarm, pull up a loop tbl in each of the 4 sc before the foundation, pull up a loop tbl in each of the next 8 (8, 8, 12, 12, 12) sc of the foundation, pull up a loop tbl in each of the next 4 sc past the underarm*; repeat from * to * once; work as Lp Even to the last 4 sc, according to your size end as Lp Inc-Neck (Lp Even, Lp Inc-Neck, Lp Inc-Neck, Lp Inc-Neck, Lp Even)—148 (156, 180, 188, 204, 212) loops.

C ROW 1 Work C Even—37 (39, 45, 47, 51, 53) groups; 148 (156, 180, 188, 204, 212) sc.

LP ROW 2 Begin as Lp Even (Lp Inc-Neck, Lp Even, Lp Even, Lp Even, Lp Inc-Neck); work Lp Even across; end as Lp Even (Lp Inc-Neck, Lp Even, Lp Even, Lp Even, Lp Inc-Neck)—148 (164, 180, 188, 204, 220) loops.

C ROW 2 Work C Even—37 (41, 45, 47, 51, 55) groups; 148 (156, 180, 188, 204, 212) sc.

LP/C ROWS 3–7 Work [Lp Even, C Even] for 5 times.

LP ROW 8 Work Lp Even.

C ROW 8 Gather the edge slightly by making [3 sc in each group of 4 loops]—111 (123, 135, 141, 153, 165) sc.

Fit Tip

Lengthen or shorten the body above the waistband by adding or omitting sets of Broomstick rows here. If you'd prefer a straight-sided, unshaped body, simply omit the waistband and continue working Lp/C Even for the length desired, end by working a Lp Even, then finish with edging.

Waistband

Turn, WS now facing, and begin cluster stitch band.

ROW 1 (WS) Ch 1, sc2tog in the first 2 sc, [ch 1, sc2tog in the next 2 sc] 54 (60, 66, 69, 75, 81) times, end with ch 1, sc in the last sc, turn—55 (61, 67, 70, 76, 82) ch-1 sps.

ROW 2 Ch 1, skip the first sc, insert hook in the first ch-1 sp to begin the first cluster, [Cl, ch 1] across, end with sc2tog in (last ch-1 sp and last sc), ch 1, sc in the last sc, turn—55 (61, 67, 70, 76, 82) ch-1 sps.

ROWS 3–5 Repeat Row 2 for 3 times, turn.

ROW 6 (RS) Ch 1, sc in the first sc, [sc in the next ch-1 sp, sc in the next sc] across—111 (123, 135, 141, 153, 165) sc.

Peplum

Turn, place the last loop onto the stick and return to Broomstick pattern, pulling up extra loops in Row 1 to shape a slight flare for the hip.

LP ROW 1 Begin with one loop on stick, skip the first sc, pull up a loop tbl in each of the next 1 (3, 5, 6, 8, 10) sc, [pull up a loop tbl in the next sc, (pull up a loop tbl, pull up a loop tfl) in the next sc] 53 (57, 61, 63, 67, 71) times, end with pull up a loop tbl in each of the last 3 (5, 7, 8, 10, 12) sc—164 (180, 196, 204, 220, 236) loops.

C ROW 1 Work C Even—41 (45, 49, 51, 55, 59) groups; 164 (180, 196, 204, 220, 236) sc.

LP/C ROWS 2–4 Work [Lp Even, C Even] for 3 times.

LP ROW 5 Work Lp Even.

Fit Tip

Lengthen or shorten here before finishing with edging. Add or omit rows, end by working a Lp Even.

Scallop Edging

With RS still facing, make edging around the entire outer edge of the vest, adding or omitting scallop repeats along the fronts if you have altered the length of the body.

EDGING ROUND Ch 1, (sc, ch 3, sc) in each group of 4 loops across the last loop row, rotate and work across row ends of the right-hand front, ch 4, [skip the loop row edge, (sl st, ch 3, dc) for a scallop in the next sc row edge] 5 times, skip the next 2 sc row edges of the band, scallop in the next sc row edge, skip the next 2 sc row edges of the band, scallop in the next sc row edge; repeat between [ ] across to the neck foundation, skip the last loop row edge before neck foundation, (scallop in the next ch of neck foundation, skip the next 3 ch) across back neck to the last 3 chs, skip the next 2 ch, scallop in the last ch; make edging along the left-hand front the same as before, end with a sl st in the last sc row edge, ch 4, sl st in the beginning sc, fasten off.

Armbands

It will take a bit of juggling to pull up loops all around the circumference of the armholes. If you have two of the same sticks, great. Pull half the sleeve loops with one stick, half the loops with the second stick. If you don't have two of the same sticks or only have one, you can still manage. Pull half the armhole loops, slip them onto a stitch holder or marker yarn, and use the same stick to pull the rest of the loops. Crochet the loops off the stick, then crochet the loops right from the marker or stitch holder. It'll be fine.

The armband is worked to a firmer gauge than the waistband; switch to the smaller, H-8 (5mm) hook if needed.

With RS facing, secure yarn tbl of the 8th (8th, 8th, 12th, 12th, 12th) (last) ch of one underarm foundation, ch 1, place the loop onto the stick.

LP RND 1 Skip the same foundation ch, pull up a loop tbl in each of the next 7 (7, 7, 11, 11, 11) ch, pull up a loop tbl in each of the next 44 (44, 52, 52, 60, 60) sc around the armhole—52 (52, 60, 64, 72, 72) loops.

C RND 1 [4 sc in the next group of 4 loops] 13 (13, 15, 16, 18, 18) times, sl st in the beginning sc, turn.

RND 2 (WS) Ch 1, [sc2tog in the next 2 sc, ch 1] around, end with sl st in the beginning sc, turn—26 (26, 30, 32, 36, 36) ch-1 sps.

RND 3 (RS) Ch 1, insert hook in the first ch-1 sp, [Cl, ch 1] around, end with sl st in the beginning sc, turn.

RNDS 4–5 Repeat Rnd 3, fasten off.

Weave in ends, block vest. Use the spaces created by the two scallops on the front edge of the waistband as button loops. Sew buttons on the waistband at the left-hand front, centered under the scallop loops of the right-hand front.

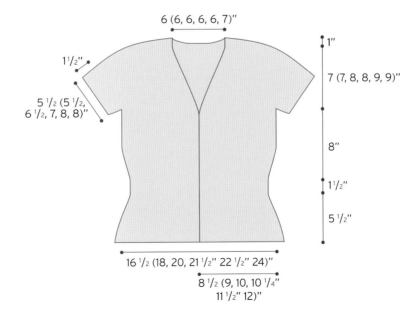

6 (6, 6, 6, 7)"

1 1/2"

5 1/2 (5 1/2, 6 1/2, 7, 8, 8)"

1"

7 (7, 8, 8, 9, 9)"

8"

1 1/2"

5 1/2"

16 1/2 (18, 20, 21 1/2" 22 1/2" 24)"

8 1/2 (9, 10, 10 1/4"
11 1/2" 12)"

JADZIA JACKET

WITH THE TEMPLATE FROM JACKET 101 (PAGE 120) AS YOUR GUIDE, CREATE A SHORT-SLEEVED, FIT-AND-FLATTER CARDIGAN, THEN USE YOUR BROOMSTICK LACE SKILLS TO ADD A LACY COLLAR. THIS YARN IS A LOVELY, LIGHTWEIGHT DK AND HAS TO BE WORKED VERY RELAXED IN ORDER TO MATCH GAUGE. AT FIRST THE FABRIC WILL SEEM TOO LOOSE, BUT, AFTER BLOCKING, THE FIBERS BULK UP SLIGHTLY TO GIVE THIS JACKET A FLOWING, NON-CLING DRAPE.

THE FRONT BANDS PROVIDE SPACES TO USE AS BUTTONHOLES. BECAUSE THIS FABRIC IS SO RELAXED, THE HOLES IN THE BAND ARE FAIRLY LARGE AND LOOSE, SO YOU'LL NEED GOOD-SIZED BUTTONS. BEWARE, THOUGH. TOO MANY HEAVY BUTTONS WILL MAKE THE FRONT REALLY SAG. CHOOSE THE LIGHTEST-WEIGHT BUTTONS YOU CAN FIND THAT ARE BIG ENOUGH NOT TO POP OUT OF THE HOLES.

SKILL LEVEL: EXPERIENCED ✦ ✦ ✦ ✦

SIZE
XS (S, M, L, XL, 2XL, 3XL); finished bust 33 (36, 39, 42, 45, 48, 51)" (84 [91, 99, 106.5, 114, 122, 129.5]cm) to fit body bust up to 34 (37, 40, 43, 46, 49, 52)" (86 [94, 101.5, 109, 117, 124.5, 132] cm) with a bit of negative ease; sample shown is size XS

MATERIALS
Lanaknits Hemp For Knitting Cashmere Canapa; 30% cashmere, 10% hemp, 60% cotton; 1.75 oz (50g)/120 yd (110m) [3]

—5 (6, 6, 7, 8, 9, 10) balls in #030 Latte

Size I-9 (5.5mm) crochet hook

Size 35 (19mm) knitting needle, 14" (35.5mm) long

Split-ring markers or contrasting yarn for markers

Buttons, at least ¾" (2cm) diameter, five or as many as desired

Needle and matching thread or self yarn for sewing buttons

GAUGE (AS CROCHETED)
11 Fsc or sc = 4" (10cm)

In shell stitch pattern, 2 repeats of (shell, sc) = 3" (7.5cm), 4 rows = 2¼" (5.5cm) (will lengthen with blocking to 2½" [6.5cm] or more)

In Broomstick lace of collar, 4 groups of 5 loops with 5 sc in each group = 4½" (11.5cm); 3 times (Loop row, sc row) = 3" (6.5cm)

STITCHES USED
Fsc (see page 134 for technique), sl st, ch, sc, hdc, dc

STITCH DEFINITIONS
SH (SHELL) (dc, ch 1, dc, ch 1, dc) all in the same stitch or space.

INC-SH (INCREASE SHELL) (dc, ch 1, dc, ch 1, dc, ch 1, dc) all in the same stitch or space.

STITCH PATTERNS
For Basic Shell Stitch Patterns and the ways to increase and decrease in rows and in rounds, see the explanations in Jacket 101 (page 120).

For more about basic Broomstick technique, see Broomstick Tutorial (page 14).

This pattern uses five loops per group, with five sc in each group.

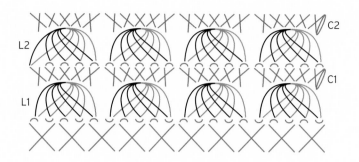

INSTRUCTIONS

Yoke

ROWS 1–11 (12, 12, 13, 13, 14, 14) Make in the same way as Jacket 101 (page 120) yoke Rows 1–11 (12, 12, 13, 13, 14, 14).

Body

ROWS 1–5 Make in the same way as the Jacket 101 Body (page 125) through joining at underarms, inserting the wedge for bust shaping if desired, completing V-Neck shaping, end by working as Patt A (B, A, B, A, B, B)—22 shells (23 shells plus half-shells at ends, 26 shells, 27 shells plus half-shells at ends, 30 shells, 31 shells plus half-shells at ends, 33 shells plus half-shells at ends).

ROW 6 Work one more row even as Patt B (A, B, A, B, A, A).

Sizes XS (M, L, 2XL) Only

ROW 7 Work one more row even as Patt A (A, B, B).

Fit Tip

To lower or raise the placement of the waist shaping, add or omit rows here, end by working a Patt A (A, A, B, B, B, A).

The Nip

See Jacket 101 (page 120) for more information about the Nip and for pattern rows used in decreasing. Mark the ch-sp at the center of the decrease points and move or wrap markers up as you go, continuing markers through completion of the flare hip shaping.

ROW 1 Begin as Patt B (B, B, A, A, A, B), work in shell stitch pattern for 2 (2, 2, 3, 3, 3) whole shells, *sc in the 2nd dc of the next shell, [dc, ch 1, dc] in the next sc for decrease; work in shell stitch pattern for 4 (5, 6, 6, 7, 8, 8) shells, sc in the 2nd dc of the next shell, [dc, ch 1, dc] in the next sc for a decrease*; work in shell stitch pattern for 5

(5, 5, 6, 6, 6, 7) shells across the back; repeat from * to * once; work in shell stitch pattern to the end, end as Patt B (B, B, A, A, A, B), turn.

ROW 2 Begin as Patt A (A, A, B, B, B, A); work over decrease points as Patt K; end as Patt A (A, A, B, B, B, A).

ROW 3 Begin as Patt B (B, B, A, A, A, B); work over decrease points as Patt L; end as Patt B (B, B, A, A, A, B)—17 shells plus half-shells at ends (19 shells plus half-shells at ends, 21 shells plus half-shells at ends, 24 shells, 26 shells, 28 shells, 29 shells plus half-shells at ends).

ROWS 4–11 Work 8 rows even in shell stitch pattern; there is a sc at the marker points of the shaping line.

Fit Tip

To lower or raise the placement of the flare hip shaping, add or omit rows here, end by working a Patt B (B, B, A, A, A, B).

The Flare

Put back four shell stitch patterns by increasing at each of the four marker points (corner sc).

ROW 12 Begin as Patt A (A, A, B, B, B, A); increase over the marked corner sc as Patt F; end as Patt A (A, A, B, B, B, A).

ROW 13 Begin as Patt B (B, B, A, A, A, B); work even corners as Patt H; end as Patt B (B, B, A, A, A, B).

ROW 14–18 (18, 18, 17, 19, 19, 20) Work even in shell stitch pattern for 5 (5, 5, 4, 5, 5, 6) more rows or to the length desired, end by working as Patt B.

Body Band

This band, similar to the drawstring waistband of Skirt 101 (page 133), offers spaces between stitches that may be used as buttonholes for optional buttons. If you have altered the length of your jacket, no worries. The exact stitch count is not critical and not given. There should be an odd number between lower corners across the bottom, and an odd number between lower corners across the fronts.

The last row of the body is now WS, turn.

RND 1 (RS) Ch 1, 2 sc in the first dc, sc in the next ch-1 sp, sc in the next dc, [skip sc, (sc in the next dc, sc in the next ch-1 sp) 2 times, sc in the next dc] 21 (23, 25, 27, 29, 31, 33) times, skip the next sc, sc in the next dc, sc in the last ch-1 sp, 3 sc in the 3rd ch of tch for the corner (mark the middle sc of the corner), rotate. Along the row edges of the right-hand front, make [2 sc in each dc row edge, sc in each sc row edge] as they appear, sc in each ch of the neck foundation, sc across the row edges of the left-hand front the same way as before, end with 2 sc in the last dc row edge, sc in the top of the same dc as at the beginning, sl st in the beginning sc, turn.

RND 2 (WS) Ch 2, hdc in the same sc, [skip the next sc, 2 hdc in the next sc] around, skip the sc before the marker, make a corner of 3 hdc in the marked corner sc (move the marker to the middle hdc of the corner), [skip the next sc, 2 hdc in the next sc] around, skip the last sc, end with hdc in the same sc as in the beginning, sl st in the 2nd ch of the beginning ch, turn.

ROW 3 (RS) Ch 1, 2 sc in the same st, sc in each hdc across, make 3 sc in the marked corner hdc, end with sc in the same stitch as at the beginning, sl st in the beginning sc, fasten off.

Short Sleeves

Fit Tip

See the template for Jacket 101 sleeves (page 126) for suggestions if you want to make long sleeves instead.

In order to tame the spread that naturally occurs at the bottom of shell fabric, taper the sleeves at the underarm one time.

All Sizes

RND 1 Make in the same way as Jacket 101 Sleeves Rnd 1 (page 123)—8 (9, 9, 10, 10, 11, 12) shells.

Sizes XS (S, M, L, XL, 2XL)

RNDS 2–5 Work Patt M, Patt O, Patt P, Patt Q, Patt N for sleeve taper—7 (8, 8, 9, 9, 10) shells.

Size 3XL

RNDS 2–6 Work Patt O, Patt P, Patt Q, Patt N, Patt M, Patt N for sleeve taper—11 shells.

Armbands

With RS facing (according to RS of the front band), make a band around the sleeve working to a slightly firmer gauge of 12 sts = 4" (10cm).

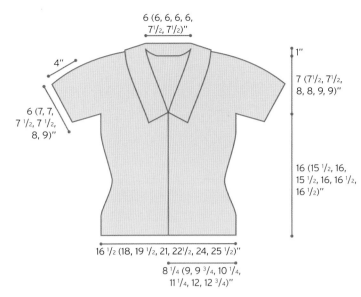

6 (6, 6, 6, 6, 7½, 7½)"

4"

1"

7 (7½, 7½, 8, 8, 9, 9)"

6 (7, 7, 7½, 7½, 8, 9)"

16 (15½, 16, 15½, 16, 16½, 16½)"

16½ (18, 19½, 21, 22½, 24, 25½)"

8¼ (9, 9¾, 10¼, 11¼, 12, 12¾)"

RND 1 (RS) Ch 1, sc in the first dc, sc in the next ch-1 sp, sc in the next dc, [skip the next sc, (sc in the next dc, sc in the next ch-1 sp) 2 times, sc in the next dc] 6 (7, 7, 8, 8, 9, 10) times, skip the next sc, sc in the next dc, sc in the last ch-1 sp, sl st in the beginning sc, turn—35 (40, 40, 45, 45, 50, 55) sc.

RND 2 (WS) Ch 2 (does not count), skip the same sc, [skip the next sc, 2 hdc in the next sc] 17 (19, 19, 22, 22, 24, 27) times, end with hdc in the same sc as at the beginning, sl st in the 2nd ch of the beginning ch, turn—35 (39, 39, 45, 45, 49, 55) hdc.

RND 3 (RS) Ch 1, sc in the next hdc, sc in each hdc around, skip beginning ch-2, end with a sl st in top of the next hdc, fasten off—35 (39, 39, 45, 45, 49, 55) sc.

Make a sleeve and armband around the other armhole in the same way.

Collar

Locate the sc at dead center of the back neck.. With WS facing, not counting center back sc, skip the next 31 sc of the front band, secure yarn in the next sc, begin making first Broomstick Loop row from left to right.

L(OOP) ROW 1 Insert hook through the front loop of the same sc, draw up a loop and put it on the stick, pull up a loop tbl in the same sc, put it on the stick, [pull up a loop tfl, pull up a loop tbl] in each of the next 64 sc—130 loops.

C(ROCHET) ROW 1 5 sc in each group of 5 loops—130 sc; 26 groups of 5 each.

LP ROW 2 Pull up loop tbl of each sc.

C ROW 2 5 sc in each group of 5 loops.

LP ROW 3 Repeat Lp Row 2 once more.

C ROW 3 Repeat C Row 2 once more, fasten off.

Sew as many buttons as desired on the left-hand side of the front band, evenly spaced and matched to openings between stitches in the right-hand front band.

Weave in ends, block jacket.

Hairpin Lace

One Hook, One Loom

THE MOST DELICATE LACE I'VE EVER SEEN WAS MADE WITH gossamer threads on a Hairpin loom. Historically, lace-makers used their U-shaped metal hairpins, sometimes called staples, as tiny tools to produce extremely fine lace. Modern Hairpin looms, found not in your hair but wherever crochet tools are sold, are adjustable and can be used with any weight yarns to make open, airy garments, accessories, items for the home, and trims.

Hairpin Lace satisfies the two sides of our dual crochet personality. There's the soothing, repetitive, fairly mechanical task of creating strips of umpteen loops on the Hairpin loom, followed by the wildly unpredictable, expressive process of joining the strips into fabric. I can only give you a snapshot of one way to make and join Hairpin strips, but I hope you will fall in love with this technique, as I have, and seek out more information.

HAIRPIN TUTORIAL

Hairpin fabric starts with long strips that are later edged or joined in various ways. Running along the center of the strip is a line of normal crochet stitches, called the spine. Any crochet stitches or combination of stitches may be used in a spine; for the strips used in the following designs you will make (ch 1, sc). On either side of the spine are loops. Loops are counted in pairs, so a strip that is 40 loops long contains 40 loops on the left side and 40 loops on the right side of the spine. Generally, the wider the loom, the longer the loops, the lacier the fabric.

Parts of the Hairpin loom are spacer bars at top and bottom with holes for holding the loom at different widths and two side pins. Helpful materials are: markers, blunt needle, and lengths of contrast yarn for lifelines.

You will be given a specific loom width in the pattern instructions. Adjust pins in the spacer bar holes to the width required (for example, 2½" [6.5cm] for stole, 3" [7.5cm] for skirt).

MAKING HAIRPIN STRIPS

1. Make a slip knot, "lasso" around the bottom of the loom, with the knot and the feeder yarn in the back and kept as close to the center of the pins as possible (a).

2. Insert hook under both strands of the lasso, YO and draw up a loop (b).

3. Ch 1 (c).

4. Sc through the front loop only of the left-hand side of the lasso (d).

5. Rotate the hook so the handle points up and the hook points down (counterclockwise), flip the handle through the middle between the pins to the back of work (e).

6. Turn the loom as you would turn the page of a book, bringing the right-hand side toward you and swinging it to the left (f).

7. Ch 1, sctfl, flip the hook, turn the loom. Repeat for the number of loops required. Slide the loops toward the bottom of the loom as you go in order to leave room for flipping the hook.

REMOVING THE STRIP

These designs require fairly short strips compared to typical Hairpin lace projects. For really long strips, you'll need to empty the loom when it gets too crowded. Remove the bottom spacer bar, slip off most of the loops (leaving the top few), replace the spacer bar, then continue to make the strip.

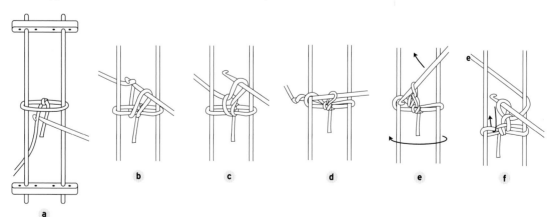

After completing a strip, pull the last loop on the hook through the final stitch as you would normally fasten off crochet. The last sc made is the top (or tip) of the strip and it also the right side. If you will not be continuing with the same yarn, cut the yarn and mark the top loops of the last sc made.

Depending on the type and twist of the yarn and how kinky it was in the skein, your loops may look like a horrible mess when the strip comes off the loom. At first you may want markers and lifelines to help keep the loops and strips from getting all twisted. Some people find the extra strands and loose ends distracting and annoying. Try it first with the markers and lifelines; later you may find you don't need these reminders.

Insert the lifeline before removing any loops from the loom. For each strip, have a 24" (61cm) or so length of lifeline yarn; any smooth contrasting color yarn or thread will work. Thread the lifeline yarn onto a blunt yarn needle. I like ball end needles for this task. Starting from the top left, slip the needle down through all the front loops on the left side. Following the path of the pin, draw the lifeline halfway through, careful not to let the tail pull through the first loop. Slip the needle up through all the front loops on the right side. Again, following the path of the pin, draw the lifeline through and remove the needle. You have the two loose ends of the lifeline at the top of the strip and a closed loop of lifeline at the bottom of the strip.

Pull off one of the spacer bars (for short strips like this it doesn't really matter which one) and slide the strip off the pins, again being careful not to pull out your lifeline.

tips for success

To keep the spine as neat and stable as possible, I now recommend a smaller-size hook than I would normally use with the yarn. For example, I routinely work worsted yarn with an I-9 (5.5mm) or a J-10 (6mm) crochet hook; for Hairpin I'd switch to a G-7 (4.5mm) or an H-8 (5mm).

I like to mark the upper left-hand hole of the spacer bar. Set up the loom and begin each strip with the marker in this starting position. Then when you finish the last stitch of your strip with the marker at the starting position you will always have an equal number of loops on each side of the strip.

If you are making a gang of strips first in order to work them later, don't ball them up and throw them around. Please put them aside in a safe stack where they won't be disturbed. See individual patterns for specific instructions on turning your Hairpin strips into fabric with edging and joining.

SIONA STOLE

• ———— •• ✦ •• ———— •

MAKING STRIPS OF HAIRPIN LOOPS IS THE EASY PART, ONCE YOU GET THE FEEL OF IT. THIS DESIGN USES SHORT, DOABLE STRIPS AS PRACTICED IN THE HAIRPIN TUTORIAL (PAGE 34). THE MORE EXACTING AND OCCASIONALLY EXASPERATING PROCEDURE COMES NEXT—ASSEMBLING THAT LOOPY PILE INTO FABRIC. THERE ARE SO MANY TECHNIQUES FOR WORKING WITH HAIRPIN STRIPS THAT I CAN'T BEGIN TO TOUCH ON THEM ALL. WHAT I WILL DO IS ILLUSTRATE AND DESIGN WITH MY FAVORITE HAIRPIN JOIN, ONE I CALL "BUBBLE" EDGING.

THE STAGGERED ASSEMBLY OF THE STRIPS IS WHAT GIVES THIS STOLE AN INTERESTING BIASED FABRIC AND A STAY-PUT FIT AROUND YOUR SHOULDERS. I'VE CHOSEN A TWO-COLOR SCHEME OF ONE SOLID PALE AND ONE SOLID DARKER SHADE, BUT YOU CAN USE ONE COLOR OR AS MANY COLORS AND YARNS AS YOU LIKE.

SKILL LEVEL: INTERMEDIATE ✦ ✦ ✦ ✦

SIZE
16" (40.5cm) back length, 72" (183cm) front edge length, 13" (33cm) wide each front; length and width adjustable

MATERIALS
Moda Dea Bamboo Wool; 55% rayon from bamboo, 45% wool; 2.8 oz (80g)/145 yd (133m) (medium weight worsted) (4)

—3 balls in #3620 Celery (MC)

—3 balls in #3650 Bamboo (CC)

Size H-8 (5mm) crochet hook

Hairpin loom, pins set to 2½" (6.5cm) width

GAUGE (APPROXIMATE)
Hairpin Module, one bubble = 2½" (6.5cm) tall, 1½" (3.8cm) wide; one module with 10 bubbles is 2½" (6.5cm) tall, 16" (40.5cm) long

STITCHES USED
Sl st, ch, sc, dc

STITCH DEFINITIONS
PICOT Ch 3, insert the hook from top to bottom through the front loop of the sc just made AND through one forward strand of the stem of the same sc (in other words, retrace the path of the last loop of the sc, going under two strands), make sl st to close Picot.

For more about making basic Hairpin strips, see the Hairpin Tutorial (page 34).

BUBBLE EDGING
This edging is made in regular crochet stitches around a strip of Hairpin loops, at the same time forming groups of loops, separating the groups into "bubbles" and connecting modules into fabric. You can continue with the same yarn you used in the strips, or change yarns, as I've done in this stole. I have suggested using a smaller hook when making strips, to keep the spine tidy, but for some projects, this edging might require a larger hook in order to get the gauge, usually the same one used in the rest of the garment. For this design, continue with the hook used for the strips, H-8 (5mm), to make modules that are flexible yet not too loose or lacy.

—Make a strip of 50 loops, fasten off yarn, insert lifeline if desired, remove the strip from the loom.

The last sc made is the tip of the strip and is now RS. This is not critical if you are planning to fasten off and begin with new yarn for the edging. But I appreciate looking at the strips in the same way each time.

—With RS facing, join yarn in the last sc at the tip of the spine, ch 1, sc in the same sc, Picot, ch 6, holding the first 5 Hairpin loops together as one, insert the hook and sc through the group of 5 loops, Picot, ch 4. Dc into the spine between the group of 5 just made and the next loop.

You may have to gently spread the stitches of the spine in order to find the "sweet spot," located just before the next "nub" of the spine. Try to find a place that is relatively stable, insert the hook under two strands to make dc. Try to do it in the same spot each time.

—[Ch 4, insert hook through the next group of 5 loops, sc, ch 4, dc in the spine] 8 times across the strip, sc through the last group of 5 loops—10 bubbles.

—At the end of the strip, ch 6, sc into the tip of the spine, again trying to locate a "sweet spot" that is stable, Picot, ch 6, rotate the strip.

—Now working across loops on the other side of the strip, [sc through the next group of 5 loops, ch 4, dc in the spine at the same place as previous dc, ch 4] 9 times, sc through the last group of 5 loops, ch 6, sl st in the beginning sc, fasten off.

—Modules are joined at the sc at the top of the groups. After making the sc through the next group of 5 loops, sl st in the corresponding sc of the previous module (or in place as directed), ch 4, continue with edging.

INSTRUCTIONS

The Siona Stole is constructed of 24 modules joined as you go. To achieve the wide V shape, the modules are assembled in a staggered column, beginning at the bottom of the right-hand side, leaning one way going toward the back neck, then leaning the other way going away from the back neck and down the left-hand side (see assembly diagram on opposite page). Modules are assembled with RS always facing. To keep this project portable for as long as possible, make all the strips with MC first. Be careful to store them neatly and mark the last sc of each strip for RS if needed.

On Hairpin loom with pins set at 2½" (6.5cm) width, using H-8 (5mm) hook and MC, make 24 strips of 50 loops each.

ASSEMBLY

Finish each strip in turn with Bubble edging in CC and assemble the modules together as you go. The first and last modules are different, and have Picot trim along the outside edge.

Module 1

Make Bubble edging with Picot at the beginning tip of the spine, Picot in each of the next 10 groups, Picot at the other tip of the spine,

complete the edging as above with no Picot in 10 groups along the other side of the strip—10 bubbles.

Module 2

Hold the next strip side by side with the no-Picot edge of the previous module. With RS facing, join yarn in the last sc at the tip of the spine, ch 1, sc in the same sc, Picot, ch 6, sc through the first group of 5 loops, ch 4, dc into the spine, ch 4, sc through the next group of 5 loops, sl st in the sc of first group of the previous module, [ch 4, dc in the spine, ch 4, sc through the next group of 5 loops, sl st in the sc of the next group of the previous module] 8 times, complete the edging without joins as above.

Modules 3–12

Make Bubble edging in the same way as Module 2.
—Join the next module even, matching all groups and not staggered, for back neck.

Module 13

(Back neck) Along the first side of the strip, join with a sl st at all 10 groups to corresponding 10 groups in the previous module, complete edging without joins as above.

Module 14

Make Bubble edging through the sc through first group of 5 loops, skip the first group of the previous module, sl st in the sc of the next group of the previous module, join with a sl st at next 8 groups (to the end of the previous module), complete the last group and the remaining edging without joins as above.

Modules 15–23

Make Bubble edging in the same way as Module 14.

Module 24

Make and join Bubble edging in the same way as Module 14 for 10 groups along the first side, make edging with Picot in each group along the outside edge, completing as above, fasten off.
Weave in ends, block stole.

This module has 10 bubbles of 5 loops each. To adjust the width of this stole, you may alter the strips. Add or omit loops on the loom as desired, end with a multiple of 5 loops.

To adjust the length of this stole, assemble as many modules as desired to reach the midway point at back neck, then begin with joining as Module 13 for back neck, continue as Module 14. Make sure you will have the same number of modules on the right and left sides, finish last module with Picot in each group of outside edge.

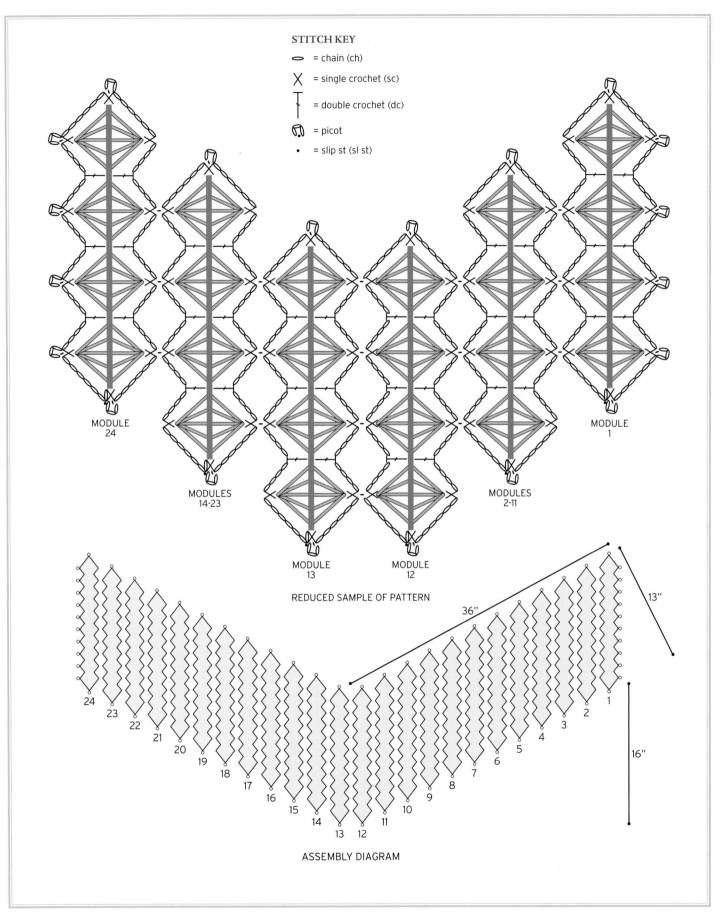

STITCH KEY

◯ = chain (ch)

✕ = single crochet (sc)

┬ = double crochet (dc)

▥ = picot

• = slip st (sl st)

MODULE 24

MODULES 14-23

MODULE 13

MODULE 12

REDUCED SAMPLE OF PATTERN

MODULES 2-11

MODULE 1

36"

13"

16"

24 23 22 21 20 19 18 17 16 15 14 13 12 11 10 9 8 7 6 5 4 3 2 1

ASSEMBLY DIAGRAM

ROHISE SKIRT

— ••◆•• —

SIMILAR TO THE MODULES USED IN THE PREVIOUS SIONA STOLE, THESE RELATIVELY SHORT, MANAGEABLE HAIRPIN STRIPS WILL BE ASSEMBLED IN A STAGGERED FASHION TO CREATE A SLANTED OR BIAS LOOK. THE STRIPS FORM A TUBE THAT ENCIRCLES THE BOTTOM OF THIS BELOW-THE-KNEE, SLIGHTLY A-LINE SKIRT. FOR A TRIM, SMOOTH SKIRT YOKE, REFER TO THE PULL-ON STYLE PRESENTED IN SKIRT 101 (PAGE 129), MADE TO MID-THIGH.

SKILL LEVEL: INTERMEDIATE ◆ ◆ ◆ ◆

SIZE

XS (S, M, L, XL, 2XL, 3XL); finished full hip 9" below waist 36 (39, 42, 45, 48, 51, 54)" (91 [99, 106.5, 114, 122, 129.5, 137]cm) to fit body hip up to 35 (38, 41, 44, 47, 50, 53)" (89 [96.5, 104, 112, 119, 127, 134.5]cm); sample shown is size XS, with no-sew elastic waist

MATERIALS

Plymouth Royal Llama Linen; 40% fine llama, 35% silk, 25% linen; 1.75 oz (50g)/109 yd (100m) (**4**)

—5 (6, 6, 7, 7, 8, 9) hanks in #1553 Berry

Size I-9 (5.5mm) crochet hook

Size H-8 (5mm) crochet hook, for use with Hairpin loom

Hairpin loom, with pins set to 3" (7.5cm) width

Split-ring stitch markers or scraps of yarn for markers

For no-sew elastic option, ⅛" (3mm) narrow braided or round elastic, cut to measure

GAUGE (AS CROCHETED)

11 Fsc or sc = 4" (10cm)

In Basic Shell Stitch Pattern, (shell, sc) 2 times = 3" (7.5cm); 4 rounds = 2¼" (5.5cm) (will lengthen with blocking to 4 rounds = 2½" [6.5cm] or more)

Hairpin Module, one bubble = 3" (7.5cm) tall, 2" (5cm) wide; one module with 8 bubbles = 3" (7.5cm) tall, 17" (43cm) long

STITCHES USED

Fsc (see page 134 for technique), sl st, ch, sc, dc

STITCH DEFINITIONS

SH (SHELL) (dc, ch 1, dc, ch 1, dc) all in the same stitch or space.

INC-SH (INCREASE SHELL) (dc, ch 1, dc, ch 1, dc, ch 1, dc) all in the same stitch or space.

PICOT Ch 3, insert hook from top to bottom through the front loop of the sc just made AND through one forward strand of the stem of the sc (in other words, retrace the path of the last loop of the sc, going under two strands), make sl st to close Picot.

For Basic Shell Stitch Pattern (in rounds), see Skirt 101 (page 129) and explanations in Jacket 101 (page 120).

For more about basic Hairpin strips, see the Hairpin Tutorial (page 34).

For Bubble edging, see explanations in Siona Stole (page 36).

INSTRUCTIONS
Skirt Yoke

RNDS 1–8 (8, 8, 9, 9, 9, 10) Make in the same way as the Skirt 101 (page 129) skirt yoke through hip shaping, Rnds 1–8 (8, 8, 9, 9, 9, 10).

Skirt Body

RNDS 9 (9, 9, 10, 10, 10, 11)–17 (17, 17, 18, 18, 18, 19) Work even in shell stitch pattern for 9 rounds, end by working as Patt M, fasten off—24 (26, 28, 30, 32, 34, 36) shells.

Fit Tip

To shorten or lengthen the skirt, do it here before you add the Hairpin modules by omitting or adding rounds [Patt N, Patt M] as desired, end by working as Patt M.

Hairpin Modules

The last round of the skirt is now RS, with a sc at the center back and 24 (26, 28, 30, 32, 34, 36) shells. Continue with RS of the skirt facing, begin connecting modules in the next shell from the center back sc. Make and assemble 12 (13, 14, 15, 16, 17, 18) Hairpin modules, joined to form a tube around the bottom of the skirt. Strips are connected from right to left to each other and to two shells of the skirt as you go, using Bubble edging (see explanation in Siona Stole, page 36), according to the assembly diagram. Edging is worked around the strip beginning at the lower tip, up one side of loops, connecting to the skirt, and back down to the lower tip.

Fit Tip

This module has 8 Bubbles of 5 loops each. To adjust the length of the skirt with the Hairpin section, you may alter the strips. Add or omit loops on the loom as desired, end with a multiple of 5 loops.

Module 1

MAKE A BASIC STRIP With the Hairpin loom set at 3" (7.5cm) and using the smaller H-8 (5mm) hook, make a strip of 40 loops with [ch 1, sc] in the spine. With RS now facing, put the last loop of the spine sc on hook on hold, insert the lifeline if desired, remove the strip from the loom.

BUBBLE EDGING With the I-9 (5.5mm) crochet hook (or the size you used for the skirt), pick up the loop on hold from the first strip. Picot in the last sc of the spine, ch 7, [sc through the next group of 5

loops, ch 5, dc in the spine, ch 5] 7 times, sc through the last group of 5 loops, **ch 7, sc in the tip of the spine, sl st in the 2nd dc of the next shell of the skirt, ch 7, rotate and work across the other side of the strip, sc through the first group of 5 loops, sl st in the 2nd dc of the next shell of the skirt, ch 5, dc in the spine, ch 5**; repeat between [ ] 6 times, sc through the last group of 5 loops, ch 7, sl st in the same sc as at the beginning, fasten off—8 bubbles.

Module 2

Make a basic strip in the same way as Module 1.
BUBBLE EDGING With the I-9 (5.5mm) hook, Picot in the last sc of the spine, ch 7, repeat between [ ] of Module 1 once, sc through the next group of 5 loops, sl st in the sc of the first group of the previous module, *ch 5, dc in the spine, ch 5, sc through the next group of 5 loops, sl st in the sc of the next group of the previous module*; repeat from * to * 5 times, repeat from ** to ** of Module 1 once to connect to the skirt, repeat between [ ] of Module 1 for 6 times, sc through the last group of 5 loops, ch 7, sl st in the same sc as at the beginning, fasten off.

Modules 3–11 (12, 13, 14, 15, 16, 17)

Make in the same way as Module 2.

Last Module

Work in the same way as the previous module through the sc in the last group of 5 loops, repeat from ** to ** of Module 1 once to connect to the skirt, [sc through the next group of 5 loops, sl st in the sc of the next group of Module 1, ch 5, dc in the spine, ch 5] 6 times, sc through the last group of 5 loops, sl st in the sc of the next group of Module 1, ch 7, sl st in the same sc as at the beginning, fasten off.

Waistband

Refer to Skirt 101 (page 129) for drawstring or elastic waist options. Make waistband desired in the same way, using 80 (88, 96, 104, 112, 120, 128) stitches of the foundation chain.
Weave in ends, block skirt.

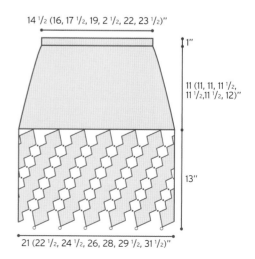

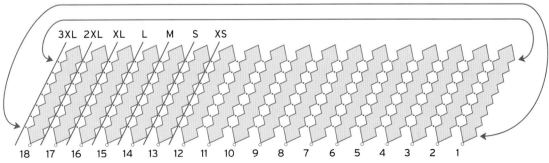

3XL 2XL XL L M S XS

18 17 16 15 14 13 12 11 10 9 8 7 6 5 4 3 2 1

KYLARA VEST

•• ✦ ••

IT IS POSSIBLE TO TAKE MY DESIGN FOR A JACKET (SEE JACKET 101, PAGE 120) AND TURN IT INTO A SLEEVELESS GARMENT SIMPLY BY OMITTING THE SLEEVES, BUT THE SHOULDERS WILL EXTEND INTO A SMALL CAP. FOR KYLARA, A TRUE SLEEVELESS VEST, WE MUST DECONSTRUCT THE JACKET TO REMOVE THE SHOULDERS AND CREATE DIFFERENT ARMHOLE PROPORTIONS TO HELP PREVENT GAPPING AT THE SIDES.

CONSIDER IT A NICE LITTLE LESSON ON GETTING A PERFECT FIT, WITH OPTIONS ALONG THE WAY FOR BUST AND WAIST SHAPING AND ALTERING THE LENGTH. BECAUSE IT IS A SMALLER PROJECT AND REQUIRES LESS COMMITMENT IN TIME AND YARN, IT IS ALSO A BRILLIANT CANVAS FOR CROCHET EXPERIMENTATION. THE BEAUTIFULLY FITTED KYLARA VEST SHOWN HERE IS OPEN-FRONT, CROPPED TO THE WAIST AND TRIMMED ALL AROUND WITH BANDS OF HAIRPIN LACE. THE SHELL STITCH PATTERN AT THE TAPERED WAIST WILL RELAX IN WIDTH AND THE HAIRPIN BUBBLES GATHERED ONTO THE EDGE WILL RELEASE INTO A LITTLE PEPLUM.

SKILL LEVEL: EXPERIENCED: ✦ ✦ ✦ ✦

SIZES
XS (S, M, L, XL, 2XL, 3XL); finished bust with front bands overlapping 33 (36, 39, 42, 45, 48, 51)" (84 [91, 99, 106.5, 122, 127]cm) to fit body bust up to 34 (37, 40, 43, 46, 49, 52)" (86 [94, 101.2, 109, 117, 124.5, 132]cm); sample shown is size XS

MATERIALS
Feza Night; 80% viscose, 2% metallic yarn; 1.75 oz (50g)/93 yd (85m) (▣)

—5 (5, 6, 7, 7, 8, 9) balls in #01 Gold

Size I-9 (5.5mm) crochet hook

Size H-8 (5mm) crochet hook, for use with Hairpin loom and modules

Hairpin loom, pins set at 2½" (6.5cm) width

Split-ring markers or scraps of yarn for markers

GAUGE (AS CROCHETED)
11 Fsc or sc = 4" (10cm)

In shell stitch pattern, 2 repeats of (shell, sc) = 3" (6.5cm), 4 rows = 2¼" (5.5cm) (will lengthen with blocking to 2½" [6.5cm] or more)

Hairpin Modules, one bubble of module = 2½" (6.5cm) tall, 2" (5cm) wide

STITCHES USED
Fsc (see page 134 for technique), sl st, ch, sc, dc, rev sc

STITCH DEFINITIONS
SH (SHELL) (dc, ch 1, dc, ch 1, dc) all in the same stitch or space.

INC-SH (INCREASE SHELL) (dc, ch 1, dc, ch 1, dc, ch 1, dc) all in the same stitch or space.

PICOT After completing a sc, ch 3, reach back and insert the hook from top to bottom through the front loop of the sc just made AND through one forward strand of the stem (in other words, retrace the path of the loop that closed the sc), YO and sl st to close Picot.

For Basic Shell Stitch Pattern rows and diagrams and the ways to increase and decrease, see Jacket 101 (page 120).

For more about basic Hairpin strips, see the Hairpin Tutorial (page 34).

For Bubble edging, see explanations in Siona Stole (page 36).

INSTRUCTIONS

This vest begins with a yoke, the same as Jacket 101 (page 120), shaping at four corners for the shoulders. Then the front and back sections are worked onto the yoke separately, with specific armhole edge shaping.

Yoke (All Sizes)

ROWS 1–3 Make in the same way as Jacket 101 (page 120) Rows 1–3.

Sizes XS (S, M)

ROW 4 Begin as Patt B; work even corners as Patt H; end as Patt B—18 (18, 19) shells plus half-shells at ends.

ROW 5 Work Patt A—19 (19, 20) shells.

Size L

ROW 4 Begin as Patt B; increase corners as Patt G; end as Patt B—19 shells plus half-shells at ends.

ROW 5 Begin as Patt A; work even corners as Patt H; end as Patt A—24 shells.

ROW 6 Work Patt C with increases at the front edges—25 shells.

Size XL

Discontinue shaping at center back, continue with four principal corners.

ROW 4 Begin with an increase as Patt C; increase corners as Patt G; end with an increase as Patt C—22 shells.

ROW 5 Begin as Patt D; work even corners as Patt H; end as Patt D—25 shells plus half-shells at ends.

ROW 6 Work Patt A—26 shells.

Sizes 2XL (3XL)

Discontinue shaping at center back, continue with four principal corners.

ROW 4 Begin with an increase as Patt C; increase corners as Patt G; end with an increase as Patt C—22 shells.

ROW 5 Begin as Patt D; increase corners as Patt G; end as Patt D—25 shells plus half-shells at ends.

ROW 6 Begin as Patt A; work even corners as Patt H; end as Patt A—30 shells.

ROW 7 Work Patt B—29 shells with half-shells at ends.

Back

Divide for Fronts and Back

If you don't mind having a second feeder yarn hanging, put the last loop on the hook at the yoke on hold. All sizes have a sc at each of the four corners, but are at different steps at the front edges.

Skip the first corner sc at the front, join yarn with sl st in the next corner sc at the start of the back.

ROW 1 Work as Patt B across, end with (dc, ch 1, dc) in the next corner sc at the end of the back, turn—6 (6, 7, 8, 9, 10, 10) shells plus half-shells at ends.

ROW 2 Work Patt A—7 (7, 8, 9, 10, 11, 11) shells.

ROW 3 Work Patt B.

ROW 4 Work Patt A.

ROW 5 Work Patt C with increases at each end—8 (8, 9, 10, 11, 12, 12) shells.

ROW 6 Work Patt E with increases at each end—9 (9, 10, 11, 12, 13, 13) shells.

Size XS

Fasten off.

Sizes S (M, L, XL, 2XL, 3XL)

ROW 7 Work Patt E with increases at each end—10 (11, 12, 13, 14, 14) shells.

Sizes S (M, L, XL, 2XL)

Fasten off.

Size 3XL

ONLY ROW 8 Work Patt E with increases at each end, fasten off—15 shells.

Fronts

Here are specific, row-by-row instructions for making front sections that will leave a 3" (7.5cm) gap between the fronts, room for the addition of a wide band. Neck edges must increase 1 (1, 2, 2, 2, 2, 2) more time(s) to complete the front edge shaping.

First Front

Sizes S (M, L, XL, 2XL) pick up the loop on hold to make the first front section.

Sizes XS (3XL) leave the loop on hold, skip the back section, join with sl st in the next corner sc at the other front.

Size XS

ROW 1 Begin as Patt B; end as Patt C with an increase at the front edge—2½ shells.

ROW 2 Begin as Patt D; end as Patt A.

ROW 3 Begin as Patt B; end as Patt A.

ROW 4 Begin as Patt B; end as Patt A.

ROW 5 Begin as Patt C with an increase at the armhole edge; end as Patt A.

ROW 6 Begin as Patt B; end as Patt E with an increase at the armhole edge, fasten off—3½ shells.

Size S

ROW 1 Begin as Patt C with an increase at the front edge; end as Patt B in the sc at the next corner, turn—2½ shells.

ROW 2 Begin as Patt A; end as Patt D.

ROW 3 Begin as Patt A; end as Patt B.

ROW 4 Begin as Patt A; end as Patt B.

ROW 5 Begin as Patt A; end as Patt C with an increase at the armhole edge.

ROW 6 Begin as Patt E with an increase at the armhole edge; end as Patt B.

ROW 7 Begin as Patt A; end as Patt E with an increase at the armhole edge, fasten off—4 shells.

Size M

ROW 1 Begin as Patt C with an increase at the front edge; end as Patt B in the sc at the next corner, turn—2½ shells.

ROW 2 Begin as Patt A; end as Patt D.

ROW 3 Begin as Patt A; end as Patt B.

ROW 4 Begin as Patt A; end as Patt B.

ROW 5 Begin as Patt A; end as Patt C with an increase at the armhole edge.

ROW 6 Begin as Patt E with an increase at the armhole edge; end as Patt C, with an increase at the front edge.

ROW 7 Begin as Patt D; end as Patt E with an increase at the armhole edge, fasten off—4½ shells.

Size L

ROW 1 Begin as Patt D; end as Patt B in the sc at the next corner, turn—2 shells with half-shells at ends.

ROW 2 Work Patt A.

ROW 3 Work Patt B.

ROW 4 Work Patt A.

ROW 5 Work Patt C with increases at each edge.

ROW 6 Begin as Patt E with an increase at the armhole edge; end as Patt D.

ROW 7 Begin as Patt A; end as Patt E with an increase at the armhole edge, fasten off—5 shells.

Size XL

ROW 1 Begin as Patt B; end as Patt B in the sc at the next corner, turn—2 shells with half-shells at ends.

ROW 2 Work Patt A.

ROW 3 Begin as Patt C with an increase at the front edge; end as Patt B.

ROW 4 Begin as Patt A; end as Patt D.

ROW 5 Begin as Patt A; end as Patt C with an increase at the armhole edge.

ROW 6 Begin as Patt E with an increase at the armhole edge; end as Patt B.

ROW 7 Begin as Patt A; end as Patt E with an increase at the armhole edge, fasten off—5 shells.

Size 2XL

ROW 1 Begin as Patt A; end as Patt B in the sc at the next corner, turn—3½ shells.

ROW 2 Begin as Patt A; end as Patt C with an increase at the front edge.

ROW 3 Begin as Patt D; end as Patt B.

ROW 4 Work Patt A.

ROW 5 Begin as Patt B; end as Patt C with an increase at the armhole edge.

ROW 6 Begin as Patt E with an increase at the armhole edge; end as Patt A.

ROW 7 Begin as Patt C with an increase at the front edge; end as Patt E with an increase at the armhole edge, fasten off—6 shells.

Size 3XL

ROW 1 Begin as Patt B; end as Patt A—3½ shells.

ROW 2 Begin as Patt C with an increase at the front edge; end as Patt A.

ROW 3 Begin as Patt B; end as Patt D.

ROW 4 Work Patt A.

ROW 5 Begin as Patt C with an increase at the armhole edge; end as Patt B.

ROW 6 Begin as Patt A; end as Patt E with an increase at the armhole edge.

ROW 7 Begin as Patt E with an increase at the armhole edge; end as Patt C with an increase at the neck edge.

ROW 8 Begin as Patt D; end as Patt E with an increase at the armhole edge, fasten off—6½ shells.

Second Front

The second front is made in the same way as the first front, reversing shaping.

Sizes XS and 3XL pick up the loop on hold at the other front.

Sizes S (M, L, XL, 2XL) join with a sl st in the sc at the other front corner.

Size XS

ROW 1 Begin as Patt C with an increase at the front edge end; end as Patt B in the sc at next corner—2½ shells.

ROW 2 Begin as Patt A; end as Patt D.

ROW 3 Begin as Patt A; end as Patt B.

ROW 4 Begin as Patt A; end as Patt B.

ROW 5 Begin as Patt A; end as Patt C with an increase at the armhole edge.

ROW 6 Begin as Patt E with an increase at the armhole edge; end as Patt B—3½ shells.

Size S

ROW 1 Begin as Patt B; end as Patt C with an increase at the front edge, turn—2½ shells.

ROW 2 Begin as Patt D; end as Patt A.

ROW 3 Begin as Patt B; end as Patt A.

ROW 4 Begin as Patt B; end as Patt A.

ROW 5 Begin as Patt C with an increase at the armhole edge; end as Patt A.

ROW 6 Begin as Patt B; end as Patt E with an increase at the armhole edge.

ROW 7 Begin as Patt E with an increase at the armhole edge; end as Patt A—4 shells.

Size M

ROW 1 Begin as Patt B; end as Patt C with an increase at the front edge—2½ shells.

ROW 2 Begin as Patt D; end as Patt A.

ROW 3 Begin as Patt B; end as Patt A.

ROW 4 Begin as Patt B; end as Patt A.

ROW 5 Begin as Patt C with an increase at the armhole edge; end as Patt A.

ROW 6 Begin as Patt C with an increase at the front edge; end as Patt E with an increase at the armhole edge.

ROW 7 Begin as Patt E with an increase at the armhole edge; end as Patt D—4½ shells.

Size L

ROW 1 Begin as Patt B; end as Patt D—2 shells with half-shells at ends.

ROW 2 Work Patt A.

ROW 3 Work Patt B.

ROW 4 Work Patt A.

ROW 5 Work Patt C, with an increase at each edge.

ROW 6 Begin as Patt E with an increase at the armhole edge; end as Patt D.

ROW 7 Begin as Patt A; end as Patt E with an increase at the armhole edge—5 shells.

Size XL

ROW 1 Work Patt B—2 shells with half-shells at ends.

ROW 2 Work Patt A.

ROW 3 Begin as Patt B; end as Patt C with an increase at the front edge.

ROW 4 Begin as Patt D; end as Patt A.

ROW 5 Begin as Patt C with an increase at the armhole edge; end as Patt A.

ROW 6 Begin as Patt B; end as Patt E with an increase at the armhole edge.

ROW 7 Begin as Patt E with an increase at the armhole edge; end as Patt A—5 shells.

Size 2XL

ROW 1 Begin as Patt B; end as Patt A—3½ shells.

ROW 2 Begin as Patt C with an increase at the front edge; end as Patt A.

ROW 3 Begin as Patt B; end as Patt D.

ROW 4 Work Patt A.

ROW 5 Begin as Patt C with an increase at the armhole edge; end as Patt B.

ROW 6 Begin as Patt A; end as Patt E with an increase at the armhole edge.

ROW 7 Begin as Patt E with an increase at the armhole edge; end as Patt C with an increase at the front edge—6 shells.

Size 3XL

ROW 1 Begin as Patt A; end as Patt B with (dc, ch 1, dc) in the sc at the next corner—3½ shells.

ROW 2 Begin as Patt A; end as Patt C with an increase at the front edge.

ROW 3 Begin as Patt D; end as Patt B.

ROW 4 Work Patt A.

ROW 5 Begin as Patt B; end as Patt C with an increase at the armhole edge.

ROW 6 Begin as Patt E with an increase at the armhole edge; end as Patt A.

ROW 7 Begin as Patt C with an increase at the neck edge; end as Patt E with an increase at the armhole edge.

ROW 8 Begin as Patt E with an increase at the armhole edge; end as Patt D—6½ shells.

Body

All sizes join front sections to back at underarms, making one continuous row by adding stitches at each underarm.

ROW 1 (JOIN UNDERARMS) Begin as Patt A (B, A, B, C, D, A), work in shell stitch pattern as established to the last shell of the front section, *sc in the 2nd dc of the shell, SH in the 3rd ch of tch, ch 1, Fsc 7 for underarm*, SH in the first dc of the back section, sc in the 2nd dc of the same shell; work in shell stitch pattern to the last shell of the back section, repeat from * to * once, work in shell stitch pattern across the front, end as Patt A (B, A, B, C, D, A), turn.

ROW 2 Begin as the Patt B (A, B, A, D, A, B), *work in shell stitch pattern as established, placing sc in the 2nd dc of the shell before the underarm foundation, SH in the first sc of the underarm, skip the next 2 sc, sc in the next sc, skip the next 2 sc, SH in the last sc of the underarm foundation, sc in the 2nd dc of the next shell*; repeat from * to * once, work in shell stitch pattern to the end, end as Patt B (A, B, A, D, A, B), turn.

NOTE After joining to the back at underarms and all stitches worked even, there should be 20 (22, 24, 26, 28, 30, 32) shells in the body.

Fit Tip

To adjust for a full bust, see Jacket 101 (page 120) for the suggestions on how and where to make the wedge before continuing, and insert your short rows where needed between the rows that follow.

Continue working even until past the fullest part of the bust, approximately 4-5" (10-12.5cm) below the underarm, inserting the wedge, if desired, between any of the next rows.

All Sizes

ROWS 3–6 Work 4 more rows even in pattern.

Sizes XS, M, L, XL Only

ROW 7 Work one more row even in pattern.

For a more relaxed vest with straight sides, stop here and see the option for an unfitted version at the end of this pattern.

Fitted Body Option

See Jacket 101 (page 120) for more about the nip and pattern rows used in decreasing.

For this fitted version, gradually nip the waist by decreasing four shell stitch patterns. Mark the ch-sp at the center of the decrease points, and move or wrap markers up as you go.

Fit Tip

Raise or lower the start of the waist shaping by omitting or adding rows here, end by working a Patt A (A, A, B, A, A, B).

ROW 1 Begin as Patt B (B, B, A, B, B, A), work in shell stitch pattern for 1 (1, 1, 2, 2, 2, 2) whole shells, *sc in the 2nd dc of the next shell, [dc, ch 1, dc] in the next sc for decrease; work in shell stitch pattern for 4 (5, 6, 6, 6, 7, 8) shells, sc in the 2nd dc of the next shell, [dc, ch 1, dc] in the next sc for decrease*; work in shell stitch pattern for 5 (5, 5, 6, 7, 7, 8) shells across back; repeat from * to *; work in shell stitch pattern to the end, end as Patt B (B, B, A, B, B, A), turn.

ROW 2 Begin as Patt A (A, A, B, A, A, B); work over decrease points as Patt K; end as Patt A (A, A, B, A, A, B).

ROW 3 Begin as Patt B (B, B, A, B, B, A); work over decrease points as Patt L; end as Patt B (B, B, A, B, B, A).

ROWS 4–11 (11, 11, 10, 11, 11, 12) Work 8 (8, 8, 7, 8, 8, 9) rows even in shell stitch pattern, all sizes end by working a Patt B—15 (17, 19, 21, 23, 25, 27) shells plus half-shells at ends.

Fit Tip

When blocked, this body of the vest, not including the band, is meant to hit just past the level of your waist. To lengthen or shorten, add or omit rows here, end by working a Patt B. You can get a better idea of the fit by doing the armhole edging now, but leaving off the front edging and the Hairpin bands. Block the unfinished vest. At that stage it will be easy to alter the bottom edge if you decide to add or rip out rows.

Edging

The last row worked is now RS. Rotate and make sc edging evenly around entire front.

EDGING ROW (RS) Ch 1, make [sc in each sc row edge, 2 sc in each dc row edge] across the row edges of the right-hand front, sc in each ch of the back neck foundation, make [sc in each sc row edge, 2 sc in each dc row edge] down the left-hand front, fasten off—117 (117, 119, 121, 127, 127, 133) sc.

Don't get too obsessive about making the exact number here. If you have altered your vest for length or inserted the Wedge bust shaping, your count will be different, but there should be the same number of sc along each of your fronts. The total should always be an odd number.

Hairpin Bands

These Hairpin modules with Bubble edging are similar to the ones used in the designs Siona (page 36) and Rohise (page 40), only longer. Even this large number of loops can fit on the loom at one time so you should not need to empty the loom. One strip is finished and connected at the same time to the front edge of the vest. A second strip is connected along the bottom.

Front Band

Some sizes will need to ease the fit of the strip onto the sc of the front edge. The bubbles are attached every 5th sc, with 2 sc left at the beginning and end of the fronts. Calculate a multiple of 5 that is less than or equal to the number of sc in your edge. That's the number of loops to make for the strip; divided by 5, that is the number of bubbles you will have in the front band.

FRONT BAND STRIP With Hairpin loom set at 2½ " (6.5cm) and H-8 (5mm) hook, make a strip of 115 (115, 115, 120, 125, 125, 130) loops, with [ch 1, sc] in the spine. With RS now facing, put the last loop of the spine sc on hook on hold, insert a lifeline if desired, remove the strip from the loom.

Bubble Edging

OUTER EDGE With RS facing, using the I-9 (5.5mm) crochet hook, pick up the loop on hold of the first strip.

Picot in the last sc of the spine, ch 7, [sc through the next group of 5 loops, Picot, ch 5, dc in the spine, ch 5] 22 (22, 22, 23, 24, 24, 25) times, sc through the last group of 5 loops, ch 7, sc in the tip of the spine, Picot, ch 7—23 (23, 23, 24, 25, 25, 26) groups of 5.

Hold the vest with RS facing, start at lower corner of left-hand front. **Any extra sc in your front edging must be eased into the assembly. The best way to handle this is to skip the extra sc somewhere along the back neck. So instead of (skip the next 4 sc of edge), do (skip the next 5 sc of edge) each time for as many extra sc as you have.**

JOINING EDGE Skip the first 2 sc of edge, [sc through the next group of 5 loops, sl st in the next sc of edge, ch 5, dc in the spine, ch 5, skip the next 4 sc of edge] 22 (22, 22, 23, 24, 24, 25) times, easing 2 (2, 4, 1, 2, 2, 3) times to fit across the extra sc of the edge, sc through the last group of 5 loops, sl st in the 3rd sc from end of the edge, (2 sc remain), ch 7, sl st in the same sc as at the beginning, fasten off—23 (23, 23, 24, 25, 25, 26) bubbles.

Bottom Band (omit for Unfitted Body Option, right)

BOTTOM BAND STRIP With Hairpin loom set at 2½" (6.5cm) and the H-8 (5mm) hook, make a strip of 95 (105, 115, 125, 135, 145, 155) loops, with [ch 1, sc] in the spine. With RS now facing, put the last loop of the spine sc on hook on hold, insert a lifeline if desired, remove the strip from the loom.

Bubble Edging

OUTER EDGE Make in the same way as the Outer Edge of the front band for 19 (21, 23, 25, 27, 29, 31) groups of 5 loops.

Hold the vest, with RS facing, start at lower corner of the right-hand front, in the Picot at the tip of the spine of the front band module.

JOINING EDGE Sc through the next group of 5 loops, sl st in Picot at the tip of the spine of the front band, ch 5, dc in the spine, ch 5, sc through the next group of 5 loops, sl st in the sc row edge of the front band edging; [ch 5, dc in the spine, ch 5, sc through the next group of 5 loops, sl st in the 2nd dc of the next shell of vest] 15 (17, 19, 21, 22, 24, 26) times; ch 5, dc in the spine, ch 5, sc through the next group of 5 loops, sl st in the sc row edge of the front band edging, ch 5, dc in the spine, ch 5, sc through last group of 5 loops, sl st in Picot at the tip of the spine of the front band, ch 7, sl st in the same sc as at the beginning, fasten off.

underarm foundation, ch 1, sc in the same ch, sc in each of the next 3 ch, 2 sc in each of the next 3 (4, 4, 4, 4, 4, 5) dc row edges, [sc in the next sc row edge, 2 sc in the next dc row edge] twice, over shell stitch pattern of the armhole make [sc in the first dc of the next shell, (sc in the next ch-1 sp, sc in the next dc) twice, skip the next sc] 4 (4, 4, 5, 5, 6, 6) times, [2 sc in the next dc row edge, sc in the next sc row edge] twice, 2 sc in each of the next 3 (4, 4, 4, 4, 4, 5) dc row edges, sc in each of the next 3 ch of the underarm, sl st in the beginning sc—51 (55, 55, 60, 60, 65, 69) sc.

ROPE TRIM (RS) Ch 1, rev sc in the same sc, [ch 1, skip the next sc, rev sc in the next sc] around the armhole. Don't worry if the count doesn't come out perfectly even for your size. If you make a rev sc in the last sc, end with a sl st in the same sc as in the beginning; if you make a rev sc in the next-to-last sc, end with ch 1, sl st in the same sc as at the beginning, fasten off.

Weave in ends, block vest.

Unfitted Body Option

You may omit the Nip waist shaping for an easy-fitting vest body. Join the fronts and back at the underarms in the same way as Body Row 1. Fill in shell stitch pattern across the underarm foundation in the same way as Body Row 2, completing all front neck shaping. Begin working even on 20 (22, 24, 26, 28, 30, 32) shell stitch pattern repeats, inserting the wedge for bust shaping on each front where needed. Then work even for the length of vest desired. Finish the front band and armholes in the same way, but omit the bottom Hairpin lace band.

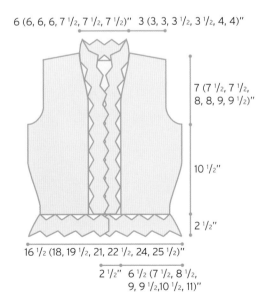

6 (6, 6, 6, 7 ½, 7 ½, 7 ½)"   3 (3, 3, 3 ½, 3 ½, 4, 4)"

7 (7 ½, 7 ½, 8, 8, 9, 9 ½)"

10 ½"

2 ½"

16 ½ (18, 19 ½, 21, 22 ½, 24, 25 ½)"

2 ½"   6 ½ (7 ½, 8 ½, 9, 9 ½, 10 ½, 11)"

Armholes

With finishing and blocking, the underarms of your vest will settle and rest comfortably deep, and the sides of the armholes should wrap around neatly with no gapping. You can adjust the fit significantly by they way you finish the armholes. A simple sc edging is all that is needed if the fit is looking good. If the arms are loose, crocheting the edging more firmly (or switching to a smaller hook if necessary) and/or adding a band or trim will snug up the opening and bring the underarm higher.

SC EDGING With RS facing, using the same hook as the vest, and working to gauge, join with sl st in the 4th ch at the center of one

Tunisian Crochet

One Long Hook

TUNISIAN (AFGHAN) CROCHET HISTORICALLY HAS HAD MANY names—Shepherd's Knitting, Scotch Knitting, Tricot Crochet, Railway Knitting, and Russian Crochet—all done with a long hook. Traditional Tunisian fabric, when made tightly using simple stitch variations, is often characterized by density (very practical for warm woolies in a cold climate) and a strong linear or gridlike quality. Wonderfully decorative, intricately artistic items can be made using this near–perfectly square grid as the ground for further embellishment, overstitching, and embroidery, rendering the fabric even denser. Once you approach Tunisian with a lace sensibility, incorporating taller stitches and holes, exploding the gauge with bigger hooks, so much more is possible.

The Tunisian hook end is exactly like a normal crochet hook of the same size. There is never a flattened grip on a Tunisian hook; it is the same diameter through the entire length with a stop or knob on the end, just like a knitting needle. Tunisian crochet is often referred to as a synthesis or a bridge between knitting and crochet because the technique requires you to have not just the one live crochet loop on the hook, but all of the stitches and all of the fabric across a row on the hook as you would in knitting. I suspect, then, that the most logical and efficient way to hold the Tunisian hook is with a knife grip. This will be awkward and annoying if you are by nature a pencil grip crocheter, and it goes a long way toward explaining why certain crocheters do not knit. I totally understand.

TUNISIAN TUTORIAL

Each row of Tunisian consists of two stages. In the first stage (forward pass) you pull up or otherwise make an entire row of loops, holding them all on the hook (resembling knitting). In the second stage (return pass) you work the loops off the hook using crochet stitches.

Tunisian hooks can be found in many of the same sizes and materials as regular crochet hooks and in different lengths. For bigger projects requiring huge numbers of stitches, there are hooks that feature a long, flexible cable like the ones in circular knitting needles. As a general guideline, you will want to use a Tunisian hook that is larger than the recommended regular crochet hook. With worsted-weight yarn I suggest practicing with a size K-10½ (6.5mm) through M-13 (9mm) Tunisian hook.

MAKING TUNISIAN FABRIC

Fsc for the needed number of stitches, turn the foundation so the sc edge is on top, begin work across the sc edge. Basic Tunisian is made with RS always facing, never turned.

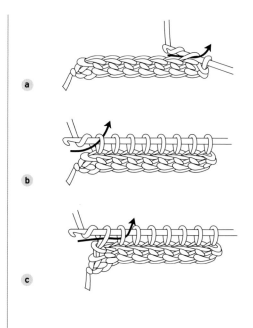

FIRST FORWARD PASS (MADE FROM RIGHT TO LEFT)

1. The loop left on hook counts as the first loop. Skip the first sc, insert hook through the back loop of the next sc (a). YO and draw up a loop, leave it on the hook (2 loops now on hook).

2. [YO and draw up a loop through the back loop] in each sc across (b).

Keep the tension even but relaxed so that the loops can slide easily on the hook.

FIRST RETURN PASS OR NORMAL RETURN (MADE FROM LEFT TO RIGHT)

3. [YO and draw through one loop on hook] to make one edge stitch.

You may want to mark that chain on the end until you get used to finding it later.

4. [YO and draw through 2 loops on hook] all the way across (c).

The last loop left on hook will begin the next forward pass.

Your loops from the forward pass are angled so that the front strand of each loop forms a vertical bar at the front of the work. Running through the center of the loops is a line of chains. Behind the line of chains is a row of back bars. The most basic fabric is made with Tunisian Simple Stitch (Tss), where the forward pass continues to be picked up through the vertical front bars.

TSS FORWARD PASS

5. Skip the first bar, insert hook from right to left under the front of the next bar (d).

6. YO and draw up a loop, leave it on the hook (2 loops now on hook) (e).

7. Insert hook and draw up a loop in each of the bars across; at the end, insert hook into the edge stitch as you would into a chain, under 2 strands (f) YO and draw up a loop.

TSS RETURN PASS

Same as normal return

GETTING FANCY

Decreases, increases, and incredibly fancy Tunisian stitches can be made by varying the place where the loops are pulled and by inserting different stitches and numbers of stitches. Generally, the more involved variations are done in the forward pass.

DECREASING IN TSS To decrease by one stitch, insert hook under the next 2 bars (g) YO and draw up one loop; work normal return.

INCREASING IN TSS (M-1) To increase one stitch, insert hook through the row, into the next space between bars and under the line of chains (h). YO and draw up a loop; work normal return.

TUNISIAN KNIT STITCH (TKS) Any crochet stitch can be done as Tunisian knit. The key is where you insert the hook when you draw up your loops in the forward pass. Each stitch has a vertical bar at the front of the work and a vertical bar at the back of the work (the bars are like a knit stitch loop). Instead of inserting the hook under the front vertical bar, as for Tss, insert hook into the knit stitch, between the front and back bars AND underneath the chain row that you made with the return pass, draw up a loop through that big space in the fabric.
To Work as Tks: Insert hook through the row into the next stitch, between the front and back strands of the loop, under the line of chains (i). YO and draw up a loop; work normal return.

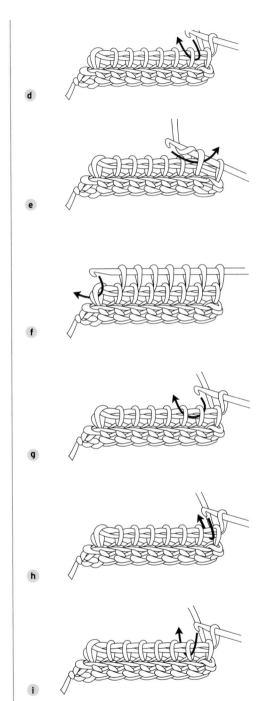

d

e

f

g

h

i

TTD (TUNISIAN TALL DOUBLE CROCHET) YO, insert hook as if to Tks in the next stitch, YO and draw up a loop, YO and draw through 2 loops on hook, ch 1, a loop remains on hook.

TSH (TUNISIAN 3-TTD SHELL) Inserting hook in stitch as if to Tks each time, 3 Ttd in the same stitch.

TUNISIAN SHELL PATTERN Here is a unique stitch pattern that will be used in all the Tunisian designs in this chapter. It is a 2-row pattern; one row of tall shells in every 3rd stitch picked up as Tunisian knit, and one row of Tss. You can make the piece as wide as you want by starting with a multiple of 3 stitches plus 2 edge stitches.

PATT Y-F(ORWARD) Ch 2 for beginning edge st, skip the vertical bar of the first stitch, skip the next st, [Tsh in the next st as if to Tks, skip the next 2 st] across (j), except after last shell skip one st, Ttd into the edge stitch.

PATT Y-R(ETURN) You have just made a Ttd that ends by ch 1. Remember to begin the return pass with another ch 1 (k), then [YO and draw through 2 loops] across (l). The stitches are very tall and the vertical bars they present are especially long.

PATT Z-F(ORWARD) Begin with one loop on hook, work as Tss, picking up one loop in each vertical bar across. At the end, the edge stitch is a bit different than the normal edge. For the last stitch, insert hook in the chain above the last Ttd, not into the chain that is part of the Ttd (m).

PATT Z-R(ETURN) Normal return.

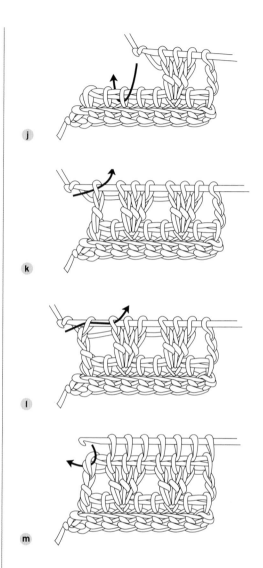

j

k

l

m

tips for success

• ◦◦ ✦ ◦◦ •

You can begin Tunisian crochet with a conventional foundation chain, inserting the hook into the chain each time. But I find that the chainless Fsc makes a better start. Making the initial stitches into the back loop of a Fsc helps tame the curl that you often get in the first rows of Tunisian.

Solid, dense Tunisian fabric can be useful, for example as the pouch part of the Scarfaroo (page 60). But for garments with drape and flexibility, the key is to loosen the gauge using larger hooks and open stitchwork.

I just love the linear aspect of Tunisian rows, the way each return row makes a textured line through the fabric. But that return pass is always the limiting factor. Chain stitches have nearly zero lateral give or stretch, so the ultimate width of your piece is determined almost exclusively by how you gauge the chains in your return pass. Try to make the chains to gauge and avoid choking up or yanking, which will make your fabric denser and tend to pucker.

On the other hand, if your return pass is loose or sloppy, it will really show on the wrong side of the fabric as irregular, messy bumps. If the wrong side is going to be seen, as in a scarf, try to keep your returns as smooth and even as possible.

For narrow projects, like the Leeloo Scarf (page 58), Scarfaroo (page 60), and Isabeau Tunisian Belt (page 102), you don't need a special Tunisian tool. If you have a regular crochet hook in the correct size that has no flattened grip—for example, a bamboo hook—feel free to use that. I pop a knitting needle point protector on the other end of the hook for security and to help keep the hook from rotating in my hand.

At the time I crocheted the samples for this chapter, I could not find affordable Tunisian hooks size L-11 (8mm) and M-13 (9mm), which are perfect for using with DK and worsted-weight yarns in the stitch patterns explored here. I used the Crochetnit tool, a double-ended hook, size M-13 (9mm), 14 inches (35.5cm) long, with caps on each end, and can be used for normal Tunisian crochet. Thanks to the lobbying efforts of the Tunisian crochet community, savvy distributors are now offering a number of alternatives to pricey custom carved hooks. See page 139 for the new tools that I have since tested and really like.

LEELOO SCARF

A SCARF IS A GOOD PROJECT FOR NAILING YOUR TUNISIAN SKILLS. SINCE IT IS NARROW, YOU DON'T NEED A SPECIAL TUNISIAN TOOL. I OFTEN USE A MAKESHIFT TOOL, A REGULAR CROCHET HOOK THE CORRECT SIZE THAT HAS AN EVEN DIAMETER THROUGHOUT THE LENGTH, LIKE A BAMBOO HOOK, WITH LITTLE FEAR OF LOOPS FALLING OFF THE END. LEELOO IS MADE IN AN OPEN, LACY TUNISIAN SHELL PATTERN, WHICH GIVES THIS WORSTED-WEIGHT ACCESSORY LOTS OF PRETTY TEXTURE WITHOUT BULK, AND SHOWS OFF THE SHIFTING COLORWAY OF THIS INCREDIBLY SOFT WOOL.

SKILL LEVEL: EASY ✦ ✦ ✦ ✦

SIZE
5½" (14cm) wide, 62" (157.5cm) long (blocked); scarf will grow narrower and longer when worn

MATERIALS
Malabrigo Kettle Dyed Pure Merino wool; 100% merino wool; 3½ oz (100g)/216 yd (200m) (4)

—One hank in #7Cadmium, or approximately 200 yd (185m) worsted-weight yarn of your choice

K-10½ (6.5mm) crochet hook

Size M-13 (9mm) Tunisian (Afghan) crochet hook or makeshift tool

GAUGE (NOT CRITICAL)
10 Fsc = 4" (10cm)

In Tunisian Shell Pattern, 4 shells = 4" (10cm), 4 rows (forward and return) = 3½" (9cm)

STITCHES USED
Fsc (see page 134 for technique), sl st, ch, sc

For stitch definitions, Tunisian Shell Pattern rows, and basic information about how to make Tunisian fabric, see the Tunisian Tutorial (page 54).

INSTRUCTIONS

Using the regular crochet hook, Fsc 17, put the last loop onto the Tunisian hook, turn the foundation so the sc edge is on top and begin work across the sc edge.

ROW 1-F(ORWARD) Same as Tutorial First Forward Pass for 17 loops, inserting hook through the back loop only of each sc—17 loops.

ROW 1-R(ETURN) Same as Tutorial First Return Pass, a normal Tunisian return.

ROW 2-F (PATT Y-F) Ch 2, skip the first vertical bar of edge stitch, skip the next st, [Tsh in the next st as if to Tks, skip the next 2 st] 5 times, except after last shell skip one st, Ttd into edge stitch—17 loops.

ROW 2-R (PATT Y-R) Normal return.

ROW 3-F (PATT Z-F) Work Tss—17 loops.

ROW 3-R (PATT Z-R) Normal return.

Work in Tunisian Shell Pattern, repeat [Patt Y (F and R), Patt Z (F and R)] for 32 times or for desired length, or until yarn runs out, leaving a yard, or meter, for finishing.

Finishing

The ending row of Tunisian crochet tends to be floppy and curls to the front. To make a neater, firmer edge for the scarf end and to more closely resemble the beginning edge, finish with a row of sc.

Place the last loop onto the regular crochet hook.

EDGING Ch 1, sc into the loop of the edge st, sc in each of the next 15 ch by inserting the hook through the back nub of the next ch of the last return pass (under one strand) each time, sc in the last edge st, fasten off—17 sc.

Weave in ends, block scarf.

STITCH KEY

⊠ = foundation sc (fsc)

⌒ = worked through back loop (tbl)

⊺ = Tunisian simple stitch (Tss)

⊘ = chain (ch)

⋎ = Tunisian 3-Ttd shell
worked as knit stitch (Tsh)

⊺ = Tunisian tall double crochet
worked as knit stitch (Ttd)

✕ = single crochet (sc)

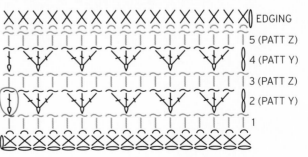

EDGING
5 (PATT Z)
4 (PATT Y)
3 (PATT Z)
2 (PATT Y)
1

NOTE: Last Ttd of row Y ends with ch 1. Remember, to begin the return
pass with another ch 1, then work [YO and draw through 2 loops] across.

SCARFAROO

— •• ✦ •• —

HANDBAGS ARE A NUISANCE. IDEALLY, I'D PREFER TO JUST SHOVE A FEW MUST-CARRY ITEMS LIKE KEYS AND WALLET INTO THE BACK POCKET OF MY PANTS, EXCEPT THAT WOMEN'S PANTS ARE OFTEN POCKETLESS. ALSO, YOU SHOULDN'T PUT HANDHELD ELECTRONICS LIKE CELL PHONES, MP3 PLAYERS, AND PORTABLE GAMES IN A PANTS POCKET IF YOU PLAN TO SIT AT ANY TIME. SO I THOUGHT TO COMBINE A POUCHY BAG, ROOMY ENOUGH FOR ESSENTIALS, WITH A COZY, ATTRACTIVE SCARF, AND CAME UP WITH THE SCARFAROO. STASH YOUR LITTLE THINGS—EVEN YOUR GLOVES, OR A JOEY IF YOU WANT—IN THE POUCH, TUCK THE POUCH UNDER YOUR ARM, TOSS THE SCARF END OVER YOUR SHOULDER, AND YOU'RE GOOD TO GO.

TUNISIAN SIMPLE STITCH (TSS) MAKES A GREAT FABRIC FOR BAGS, AS IT IS NICELY SOLID AT THIS GAUGE SO THERE'S LESS POKE-THROUGH. THE LACY SCARF USES THE SAME TUNISIAN SHELL PATTERN AS THE LEELOO SCARF (PAGE 58), FINISHED WITH SOME FLUFFY FRINGE TO BALANCE THE POUCH. AND LIKE LEELOO, SCARFAROO IS ALSO NARROW ENOUGH THAT IT DOES NOT REQUIRE A SPECIAL TUNISIAN HOOK.

SKILL LEVEL: EASY ✦ ✦ ✦ ✦

SIZE
Scarf 6" (15cm) wide, 48" (122cm) long plus fringe; attached Pouch 6" by 6" (15cm x 15cm)

MATERIALS
Red Heart Eco-Ways (E570); 70% acrylic, 30% recycled polyester; 4 oz (113g)/186 yd (170m) (4)

—2 skeins in #1615 Lichen

Size K-10½ (6.5mm) crochet hook

Size K-10½ (6.5mm) Tunisian (Afghan) crochet hook or makeshift tool

Split-ring stitch markers or scraps of yarn for markers

Large snap closure, one or two sets, for security if desired

Needle and matching thread for sewing snap closure

GAUGE (NOT CRITICAL)
In Tss, 16 st = 4" (10cm), 13 rows = 4" (10cm)

In Tunisian Shell Pattern, 3 shells = 2½" (6.5cm); 4 rows = 3" (7.5cm)

STITCHES USED
Fsc (see page 134 for technique), sl st, ch, sc, M-1

For stitch definitions, increasing (M-1) and decreasing (dec2tog) in Tss, Tunisian Shell Pattern rows, and basic information about how to make Tunisian fabric, see the Tunisian Tutorial (page 54).

INSTRUCTIONS
Cut 55 strands of yarn, 14" (35.5cm) long, for fringe.

Pouch
The pouch is made in one piece, beginning at the upper front edge, down a shaped front, worked even up the back to the upper back edge.

Using the regular crochet hook, Fsc 23, put the last loop onto the Tunisian hook, turn the foundation so the sc edge is on top and begin work across the sc edge.

ROW 1-F(ORWARD) Same as Tutorial First Forward Pass (page 54), for 23 loops, inserting hook through the back loop only of each sc—23 loops.

ROW 1-R(ETURN) Same as Tutorial First Return Pass (page 54), a normal Tunisian return.

ROWS 2–5 Work Tss for 4 rows.

Increase 5 sts across.

ROW 6-F Work as Tss, with one loop on hook, skip the first st, pick up loops in each of the next 3 bars, [M-1, pick up loops in each of the next 4 bars] 4 times, M-1, pick up loops in each of the next 2 sts, pick up in the edge st—28 loops.

ROW 6-R Normal return.

ROWS 7–10 Work Tss for 4 rows.

Increase 6 sts across.

ROW 11-F Work as Tss, with one loop on hook, skip the first st, pick up a loop in each of the next 3 bars, [M-1, pick up a loop in each of the next 4 bars] 5 times, M-1, pick up a loop in each of the next 3 bars, pick up a loop in the edge st—34 loops.

ROW 11-R Normal return.

ROWS 12–18 Work Tss for 7 rows.

Decrease 11 sts across.

ROW 19-F Work as Tss, with one loop on hook, skip the first st, [dec2tog, pick up a loop in the next bar] 10 times, dec2tog, pick up a loop in the edge st—23 loops.

ROW 19-R Normal return.

ROW 20 Work Tss.

Mark the edge st at both ends of Row 20 for a fold line at the bottom of the pouch, work even for the back of the pouch.

ROWS 21–40 Work Tss for 20 rows.

Mark the edge st at both ends of Row 40 for the upper edge of the pouch back.

ROW 41 Work Tss, fasten off.

Scarf

Turn to WS of pouch fabric. This becomes RS of the scarf. Join yarn in the edge st, begin Tunisian Shell Pattern. For the first row only, you will be working into the backs of the sts of the previous row of Tss as you work the scarf onto the pouch.

ROW 1-F Ch 2, skip the first vertical bar of the edge stitch, skip the next st, [Tsh in the next st as if to Tks, skip the next 2 st] 7 times, except after the last shell skip one st, Ttd into the edge stitch—7 shells (23 loops).

ROW 1-R Normal return.

ROWS 2–64 Work Patt Z, then repeat [Patt Y, Patt Z] 31 times or for the length desired.

Place the last loop onto the regular crochet hook.

EDGING Ch 1, sc into the loop of the edge st, sc in each of the next 21 ch by inserting hook through the back nub of the next ch of the last return pass (under one strand) each time, sc in the last edge st, fasten off—23 sc.

Finishing

Switch to the regular crochet hook. With WS of fabric together to the inside, fold the pouch in half along the fold line between markers at Row 20, matching edge stitches at each side, matching row edges of Fsc with the marked edge stitches of Row 40.

FIRST SIDE SEAM With front of the pouch facing, join yarn with a sl st in the lower fold-line marker, sl st in each of the next 19 edge sts through both thicknesses, sl st in the row edge of Fsc tog with the marked edge st at the upper edge of the pouch back, fasten off.

SECOND SIDE SEAM At the front of the pouch facing, join yarn with a sl st in the row edge of Fsc tog with the marked edge st at the other side of the upper edge, sl st in each of the next 19 edge sts through both thicknesses, sl st in the other marked edge st at the lower fold line, fasten off.

Sew snap closure(s) as desired to inside top opening of the pouch.

Weave in ends. The pouch does not really need blocking, but you may wish to block the scarf for a nicer appearance.

Fringe

Holding together 5 of the 14" (35.5cm) strands each time, skip the first sc of the scarf edging, [knot fringe in the next sc, skip the next sc] 11 times.

meglet cape

MEGLET CAPE

•———————•• ✦ ••———————•

READY FOR A TUNISIAN CROCHET GARMENT? MEGLET ADDS STITCH SHAPING TO THE TUNISIAN
SHELL PATTERN AND A WHOLE OTHER DIMENSION TO WHAT IS DOABLE WITH THE TECHNIQUE.
THIS CAPE IS AN ALMOST PERFECT HALF-CIRCLE, WITH SIX INCREASE POINTS AROUND. IN
THIS OVERSIZED GAUGE, THE FABRIC TAKES ON A SOFT, LOOSE DRAPE THAT GIVES THE CAPE A
STRETCHY FIT AND A BIT OF SWING. JUST THE RIGHT LENGTH TO COVER THE ARMS AND WAIST,
CLOSED WITH THREE BIG BUTTONS, AND TOPPED WITH A LACY COLLAR, MEGLET IS AS FUN TO
WEAR AS IT IS TO CROCHET.

SKILL LEVEL: INTERMEDIATE ✦ ✦ ✦ ✦

SIZE
Average (Large); finished lower edge 80
(97)" (203 [246]cm); finished length 20
(22)" (51 [56]cm); sample shown is size
Average

MATERIALS
NaturallyCaron.com Country; 75%
microdenier acrylic, 25% merino wool; 3
oz (85g)/185 yd (170m) (④)

—4 (6) skeins in #0021 Peacock

Size K-10½ (6.5mm) crochet hook

Size J-10 (6mm) crochet hook, for front
bands

Size M-13 (9mm) Tunisian hook

Split-ring stitch markers or scraps of
yarn for markers

Buttons, ¾" (2cm) to 1" (2.5cm)
diameter, 3 or number desired

GAUGE
9 Fsc or sc = 4" (10cm)

In firmer sc of the front bands, using
smaller hook if needed, 10 sc = 4"
(10cm)

In Tunisian Shell Pattern, 3 shells = 4"
(10cm), 4 rows (forward and return) =
3½" (9cm)

STITCHES USED
Fsc (see page 134 for technique), sl st,
ch, sc

For stitch definitions, Tunisian Shell
Pattern and stitch diagrams, and
basic information about how to make
Tunisian fabric, see the Tunisian
Tutorial (page 54).

INSTRUCTIONS
Body

By the time you get to the final few rounds, there are so many
stitches that you may encounter problems with crowding
and confusion. I can get all the loops onto a 14" (35.5cm)
long Tunisian hook, but the first loop keeps falling off the
knob end. I started using a big split-ring stitch marker or a
giant safety-pin marker, pinning through the first loop and
around the hook. The pin just fits around the size M-13
(9mm) hook and anchors the loop very efficiently. You can
also manage the large number of loops by using two hooks,
working half the stitches on one, half on the second. You
can also slip some of the loops onto stitch holders, or any

size flexible or circular hook or circular knitting needle with
a long cable.

Using the larger regular crochet hook, Fsc 41, put the last
loop onto the Tunisian hook, turn the foundation so the sc
edge is on top and begin work across the sc edge.

Size Average

ROW 1-F(ORWARD) Same as Tutorial First Forward Pass
(page 54) for 41 loops, inserting hook through the back loop
only of each sc.

ROW 1-R(ETURN) Same as Tutorial First Return Pass
(page 54), a normal Tunisian return.

ROW 2-F Ch 2, skip the first vertical bar of the edge stitch, skip the next st, [Tsh in the next st, skip the next 2 sts, 3 Tsh in the next st, skip the next 2 sts, Tsh in the next st, skip the next 2 sts] 6 times, except after the last shell skip one st, Ttd into edge st—25 shells.

ROW 2-R Normal return.

ROWS 3-F Work Tss—77 loops.

ROW 3-R Normal return.

ROWS 4–5 Work even in Tunisian Shell Pattern, as [Patt Y (F and R), Patt Z (F and R)] once.

ROW 6-F Ch 2, skip the next st, [Tsh in the next st, skip the next 2 sts] twice, *3 Tsh in the next st, skip the next 2 sts, [Tsh in the next st, skip the next 2 sts] 3 times*; repeat from * to * 5 times, except omit the last Tsh, skip one st, end with Ttd in the edge st—37 shells.

ROW 6-R Normal return.

ROWS 7–9 Work even as Patt Z, then [Patt Y, Patt Z] once.

ROW 10-F Ch 2, skip the next st, [Tsh in the next st, skip the next 2 sts] 3 times, *3 Tsh in the next st, skip the next 2 sts, [Tsh in the next st, skip the next 2 sts] 5 times*; repeat from * to * 5 times, except omit the last 2 Tsh, skip one st, end with Ttd in the edge st—49 shells.

ROW 10-R Normal return.

ROWS 11–15 Work even for 5 rows as Patt Z, then [Patt Y, Patt Z] twice.

ROW 16-F Ch 2, skip the next st, [Tsh in the next st, skip the next 2 sts] 4 times, *3 Tsh in the next st, skip the next 2 sts, [Tsh in the next st, skip the next 2 sts] 7 times*; repeat from * to * 5 times, except omit the last 3 Tsh, skip one st, end with Ttd in the edge st—61 shells.

ROW 16-R Normal return.

ROWS 17–21 Work even for 5 rows as Patt Z, then [Patt Y, Patt Z] twice.

Size Large

ROWS 1–3 Same as size Average Rows 1–3—25 shells.

ROW 4 Same as size Average Row 6—37 shells.

ROWS 5–7 Same as size Average Rows 7–9.

ROW 8 Same as size Average Row 10—49 shells.

ROWS 9–11 Repeat size Average Rows 7–9.

ROW 12 Same as size Average Row 16—61 shells.

ROWS 13–17 Same as size Average Rows 11–15.

ROW 18 Ch 2, skip the next st, [Tsh in the next st, skip the next 2 sts] 5 times, *3 Tsh in the next st, skip the next 2 sts, [Tsh in the next st, skip the next 2 sts] 9 times*; repeat from * to * 5 times, except omit the last 4 Tsh, skip one st, end with Ttd in the edge st—73 shells.

ROWS 19–23 Same as size Average Rows 17–21.

Finishing

Put the last loop onto the larger regular crochet hook, with RS still facing, make sc evenly around the entire outer edge of cape. Edging around the lower edge is more relaxed and crocheted to a gauge of 9 sc = 4" (10cm). For front edges, work more firmly, at 10 sc = 4" (10cm), switching to the smaller hook for those sections if needed.

EDGING Ch 1, sc into the loop of the edge st, sc in each ch across by inserting hook in the back nub of the ch of the last return pass, under one strand each time, 3 sc in the last edge st for the corner, mark the 2nd sc in the middle of the corner, rotate. Along the Tunisian row edges, work more firmly [sc in each Tss row edge, 4 sc in each Ttd row edge] up the right-hand front, sc in the last Tss row edge before the neck foundation, 3 sc in the first ch of the foundation, mark the 2nd sc in middle of the corner, sc in each of the next 39 chs of the foundation, 3 sc in the last ch, mark the 2nd sc in the middle of the corner, sc down the left-hand front the same way as on the other front, end with 2 sc in the same edge st as at the beginning, fasten off.

Collar

It is easier to make the collar before finishing the front bands.

With WS of the neck sc edging facing you, skip the marked middle sc of the corner, secure yarn tbl of the next sc, pull up a loop tbl of the same sc, put it on the Tunisian hook.

ROW 1-F Same as Row 1-F of Body—41 loops.

ROW 1-R Normal return.

ROW 2-F Ch 2, skip the next st, [Tsh in the next st, skip the next 2 sts] 13 times, except after the last shell skip one st, end with Ttd in the edge st—13 shells of 3 Ttd (41 loops).

ROW 2-R Normal return.

ROW 3 Work even as Patt Z.

ROW 4-F Ch 2, skip the next st, [5 Ttd in the next st, skip the next 2 sts] 13 times, except after last Ttd, skip one st, end with Ttd in the edge st—13 shells of 5 Ttd (67 loops).

ROW 4-R Normal return.

ROW 5 Work even as Patt Z.

ROW 6-F Ch 2, skip the next 2 sts, [7 Ttd in the next st, skip the next 4 st] 13 times, except after last Ttd, skip 2 sts, end with Ttd in the edge st—13 shells of 7 Ttd (93 loops).

ROW 6-R Normal return.

ROW 7 Work even as Patt Z.

Put the last loop onto the regular crochet hook.

EDGING Ch 1, sc into the loop of the edge st, sc in each of the next 91 ch by inserting hook in the back nub of the ch of the last return pass, under one strand each time, sc in the last edge st, fasten off—93 sc.

Front Bands

Use the same-size hook as you used for the front sc edging. Make 2 rows of sc on each of the fronts, working button loops on the right-hand front. I have decided that three buttons look good, but feel free to make as many as you like.

Left-hand Front Band

With WS facing, join yarn with sl st in the marked 2nd corner sc in the lower left-hand front.

ROW 1 (WS) Ch 1, sc in each sc up the front, end with a sc in the marked 2nd corner sc before the collar, turn—54 (59) sc.

ROW 2 (RS) Ch 1, sc in each sc across, fasten off.

Right-hand Front Band

With WS facing, join yarn with sl st in the marked 2nd corner sc at the upper right-hand front, just past the collar.

ROW 1 (WS) Ch 1, sc in each sc down the front, end with a sc in the marked 2nd corner sc at the bottom, turn—54 (59) sc.

ROW 2 (RS) Ch 1, sc in each of the next 37 (42) sc, [ch 4, moving from left to right backwards, skip sc just made, skip the next 2 sc, sl st in the next sc, sl st in each of 4 ch, sl st in top of the last sc made] for the button loop; sc in each of the next 8 sc, make a button loop; sc in each of the next 8 sc, make a button loop, sc in the last sc, fasten off. Sew buttons on the left-hand band, centered under loops. Weave in ends, block cape.

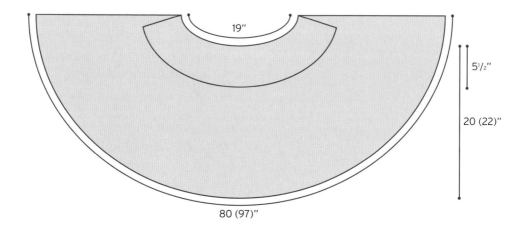

19"

5½"

20 (22)"

80 (97)"

Exploded Motifs

Gee, I'm a Tree

NOTHING SCREAMS CROCHET AS OBVIOUSLY OR AS INSISTENTLY as an afghan made with the traditional 3dc-in-each-group "granny square." It was one of the first techniques my mother taught me and I marveled at how a round could be turned into a square, and that one of them made a serviceable saddle blanket for my toy ponies. Taken beyond this humble form, the crocheted motif can be visually stunning, with many possible shapes and infinite variations. Motifs with regular shapes—squares, hexagons, octagons, and rounds—are the most typical because the geometry of putting them together is most logical. But who says you have to stick to the typical shapes? And who says all your motifs have to be the same shape throughout? Not me.

As I observed in my own home as a child, all manner of household items were painstakingly crocheted with tiny thread motifs, from tablecloths to bedspreads to antimacassars. By exploding the crochet, and enlarging the gauge and the proportions by swapping the thread and the fine steel hooks for thicker yarn and bigger hooks, the teeny motif of a traditional thread design can be beefed up with kick-butt, speedier results.

My mother didn't know about joining as you go, so she assembled all her motifs by crocheting or sewing seams or stitching individual attachments between motif points, which added an eternity and a gazillion loose ends to the project. Once I stumbled on the marvel of assembling motifs during the last round, I was enthralled. I also discovered that unexpectedly thrilling things happen when you join motifs. Wherever the corners, sides and points touch, they can form lace patterns that are not apparent when viewed individually. The whole truly is way more complex and beautiful than the sum of its parts.

ZHAAN WRAP

•———•• ✦ ••———•

D̶O̶.̶ LOVE SOCK YARN? THE COLORWAYS ARE SO EXCITING AND THE SPRINGY TEXTURE IS FUN TO WORK WITH. BUT MANY CROCHETERS SHARE MY DILEMMA. WHAT CAN YOU DO WITH SOCK YARN BESIDES MAKE SOCKS? EXPERIMENT WITH EXPLODED LACE.

IT DOESN'T TAKE A WHOLE LOT OF EXPLOSION TO GET BREATHTAKING RESULTS. I WAS IMMEDIATELY DRAWN TO THIS MOTIF FROM A VINTAGE BEDSPREAD. THE ORIGINAL THREAD DESIGN NEEDED 360 MOTIFS FOR A SINGLE BED, USING AN INSANE NINETY-NINE BALLS OF SIZE 20 THREAD. BY SWAPPING OUT THE THREAD FOR YOUR FAVORITE SOCK OR OTHER FINE YARN—NOT A HUGE JUMP—AND WITH SOME TWEAKING OF THE CHAIN SPACES IN EACH ROUND IN ORDER TO MAINTAIN THE PROPORTIONS, THIS MOTIF CAN BE EXPLODED TO DOUBLE THE ORIGINAL DIMENSIONS. NOW YOU CAN ENJOY THE FUN AND BEAUTY OF THIS EYE-CATCHING MOTIF IN NO TIME. USING ONE ORPHAN BALL OF SOCK YARN, YOU CAN MAKE ENOUGH SQUARES FOR A SCARF. WITH TWO BALLS OF YARN YOU CAN ASSEMBLE SIXTEEN SQUARES INTO A LONG RECTANGLE FOR A STOLE OR INTO A V FOR A PRETTY SHAPED WRAP, AS SHOWN IN THE SAMPLE.

PRACTICALLY ANY SQUARE MOTIF CAN BE SUCCESSFULLY EXPLODED AND ASSEMBLED IN THE SAME WAY AS ZHAAN, SO DON'T STOP WITH THE PATTERN HERE. EXPLODE YOUR OWN FAVORITE MOTIF, AND SEE IF YOU LIKE THE RESULT. THEN MAKE ENOUGH OF THEM TO PUT TOGETHER INTO A GOOD-SIZED RECTANGLE OR SHAPED V.

SKILL LEVEL: EASY ✦ ✦ ✦ ✦

SIZE
Scarf (8 motifs), 9" (23cm) wide by 72" (183cm) long (not shown); Stole (16 motifs), 18" (45.5cm) wide by 72" (183cm) long (not shown); Wrap (16 motifs), 18" (45.5cm) wide fronts, 54" (137cm) front edge length, 24" (61cm) back neck length

MATERIALS
South West Trading Company TOFUtsies; 50% Superwash wool, 25% Soysilk® fibers, 22.5% cotton, 2.5% chitin (fiber from shrimp and crab shells that is naturally antibacterial); 3½ oz (100g)/465 yd (425m) (1)

—One ball for Scarf (approx 450 yd [415m]); 2 balls for Stole or Shawl (approx 900 yd [830m])

Size G-6 (4mm) crochet hook

GAUGE
Motif, after Rnd 3 = 4" (10cm) diameter

Motif, blocked = 9" (23cm) square

STITCHES USED
sl st, ch, sc, tr

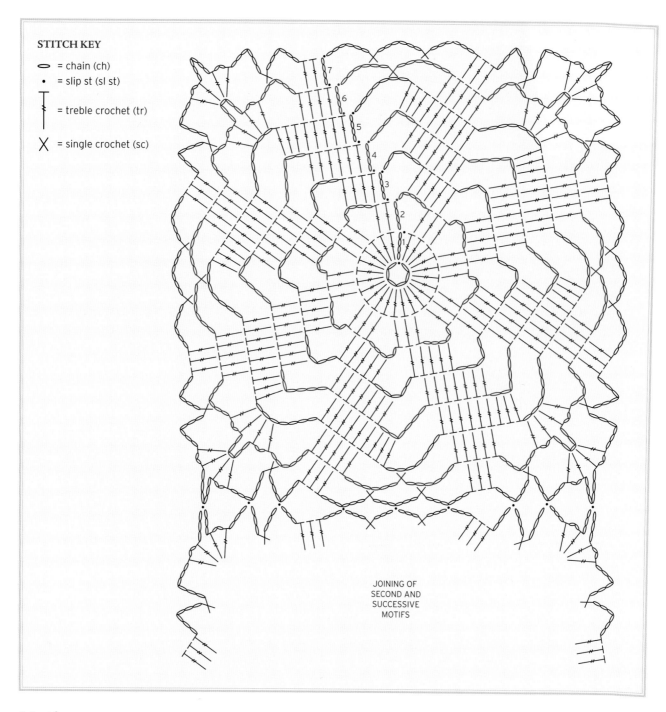

STITCH KEY

⬯ = chain (ch)

• = slip st (sl st)

⊤ = treble crochet (tr)

✕ = single crochet (sc)

JOINING OF
SECOND AND
SUCCESSIVE
MOTIFS

Motifs

—Motifs are crocheted with RS always facing and are connected to each other as you go in the last round.

—In order to keep this project portable for as long as possible, you may consider completing all the motifs separately and fastening off each one, leaving an extra-long tail. When you are ready for the task of assembly, rip out as many sides of each motif as you need and recrochet with the joins.

—To connect motifs to each other while making the last round:

JOIN Instead of a ch 6, make ch 3, sl st in corresponding ch-6 sp of the previous motif, ch 3, continue with the next stitch on the working motif.

—To join where there is already a sl st join, insert hook into the sl st of the previous join, under 2 strands, make sl st.

Basic Motif

RND 1 Ch 7, sl st in the beginning ch to form a ring. Ch 4 (counts as tr), 23 tr in the ring, sl st in the 4th ch of the beginning ch—24 tr.

RND 2 Ch 4, skip the same tr, tr in each of the next 2 tr, [ch 5, tr in each of the next 3 tr] 7 times, end with ch 5, sl st in the 4th ch of the beginning ch—8 groups of 3 tr each.

RND 3 Sl st in the next tr, ch 4, tr in the next tr, [3 tr in the next ch-5 sp, ch 5, skip the next tr, tr in each of the next 2 tr] 7 times, 3 tr in the last ch-5 sp, ch 5, sl st in the 4th ch of the beginning ch—8 groups of 5 tr each.

RND 4 Sl st in the next tr, ch 4, tr in each of the next 3 tr, [3 tr in the next ch-5 sp, ch 6, skip the next tr, tr in each of the next 4 tr] 7 times, 3 tr in the last ch-5 sp, ch 6, sl st in the 4th ch of the beginning ch—8 groups of 7 tr each.

RND 5 Sl st in the next tr, ch 4, tr in each of the next 5 tr, [3 tr in the next ch-6 sp, ch 7, skip the next tr, tr in each of the next 6 tr] 7 times, 3 tr in the last ch-6 sp, ch 7, sl st in the 4th ch of the beginning ch—8 groups of 9 tr each.

RND 6 Sl st in the next tr, tr in each of the next 4 tr, [ch 6, in the next ch-7 sp make a corner of (tr, ch 2, tr, ch 5, tr, ch 2, tr), ch 6, skip the next tr, tr in each of the next 5 tr, ch 6, sc in the next ch-7 sp, ch 6, skip the next tr, tr in each of the next 5 tr] 4 times, except omit the last 5 tr, instead end with sl st in the 4th ch of the beginning ch—8 groups of 5 tr each, with four corners.

RND 7 Sl st in the next tr, ch 4, tr in each of the next 2 tr, ch 6 **or Join**, sc in the next ch-6 sp, *ch 6 **or Join**, in the next ch-5 corner sp make (tr, ch 2, tr, ch 6 **or Join**, tr, ch 2, tr), [ch 6 **or Join**, sc in the next ch-6 sp, ch 6 **or Join**, skip the next tr, tr in each of the next 3 tr, ch 6 **or Join**, sc in the next ch-6 sp] twice*; repeat from * to * 3 times, except omit the last repeat between [ ], end with ch 6 **or Join**, sc in the last ch-6 sp, ch 6 or Join, sl st in the 4th ch of the beginning ch, fasten off.

INSTRUCTIONS

SCARF This is a simple, long rectangle. Make 8 motifs or as many as desired or until yarn runs out; assemble end to end.

STOLE This is a double-wide rectangle. Make 16 motifs; assemble into a rectangle that is 2 motifs wide by 8 motifs long.

SHAWL This is a shaped shawl with a point at the center back and arms that drape across the front. Make 16 motifs; assemble according to the diagram into a V shape.

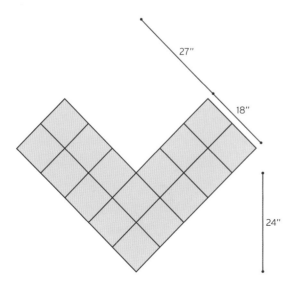

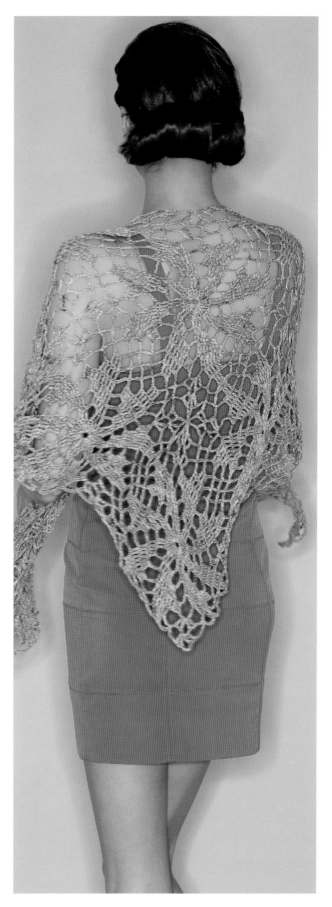

ROSALINDA TOP

— •• ✦ •• —

BORROWED FROM A VINTAGE THREAD TABLECLOTH DESIGN, THIS MOTIF ORIGINALLY HAD EIGHT "ARMS." NOW WITH AN EXTRA ARM IN A SUPER-EXPLODED GAUGE, IT MAKES A BOLD STATEMENT IN THE YOKE OF THIS PLAYFUL TOP. OFFERED IN ONE BIG, ROOMY SIZE, THIS PULLOVER ACTS MORE LIKE A PONCHO WITH EXAGGERATED SLEEVES OR WINGS. ROSALINDA IS CROCHETED IN A HAPPY COLOR, A DEEP RED TWISTED WITH A BRIGHT RED FOR A SUBTLE TWEED EFFECT. SWAP OUT THE SUPERWASH DK WOOL FOR A SUMMERY COTTON OR LINEN YARN TO EXTEND ITS SEASON.

SKILL LEVEL: INTERMEDIATE ✦ ✦ ✦ ✦

SIZE
One size fits most (up to 2XL); finished full body 49" (124.5cm); finished length 21" (53.3cm)

MATERIALS
Filatura di Crosa Zara; 100% extra fine merino Superwash wool: 1.75 oz (50g)/136 yd (125m) (3)

—9 balls in #1770 Red Chine

Size I-9 (5.5mm) crochet hook

Split-ring markers or scraps of yarn for markers

GAUGE
12 st = 4" (10cm)

In lace stitch of body, one repeat = 3½" (9cm); 4 rows in pattern = 2½" (6.5cm)

One motif = 8½" (21.5cm) diameter

STITCHES USED
Fsc (see page 134 for technique), sl st, ch, sc, hdc, dc, trtr, rev sc

STITCH DEFINITIONS
SH (SHELL) [2 dc, ch 2, 2 dc] all in the same stitch or space.

SH IN SH make SH in the ch-2 sp of the next shell.

V [dc, ch 2, dc] all in the same stitch or space.

V IN V make V in ch-2 sp of the next V.

Stitch Pattern (for body and sleeves in rounds)
PATT RND Ch 3 (counts as dc), dc in the first ch-sp, *ch 1, skip the next ch-1 sp, dc in the next ch-1 sp, ch 1, V in the next V, ch 1, dc in the next ch-1 sp, ch 1, skip the next ch-1 sp, SH in the next shell*; repeat from * to * around, except omit the last SH, instead end with 2 dc in the same ch-sp as at the beginning, ch 1, sc in the 3rd ch of the beginning ch, turn.

Basic Motif
The motif has 9 arms that are completed in sequence, with the last and first arms connected to close the motif. Motifs are joined as you go to at the tips of the corresponding arms.

When making dc over a long ch-sp, insert hook under the chain, not into the individual chains.

CENTER (RS) Ch 4, sl st in the beginning ch to form a ring, ch 3 (counts as hdc, ch 1), [hdc, ch 1] 8 times in the ring, sl st in the 2nd ch of the beginning ch, sl st in the next ch-1 sp.

ARM 1 Ch 14, mark the 4th ch from hook (the first 3 chs count as dc), dc in the 5th ch from hook, make 13 dc over the remaining ch-sp, hdc in the next ch-1 sp of the center, turn.

ARM 2 Ch 9, skip the first hdc, skip the next 6 dc, dc in the next dc, [ch 1, skip the next dc, dc in the next dc] 4 times, turn. Ch 4 or Join at the tip (counts as a dc, ch 1), [dc in the next

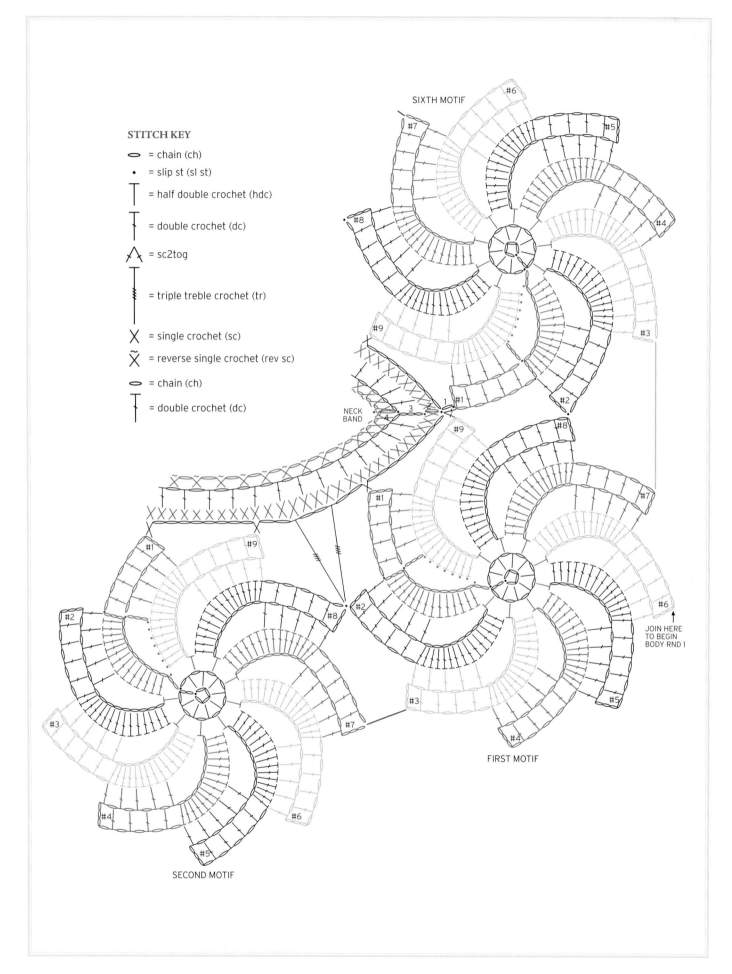

STITCH KEY

◯ = chain (ch)

• = slip st (sl st)

┬ = half double crochet (hdc)

┼ = double crochet (dc)

⋏ = sc2tog

≋ = triple treble crochet (tr)

✕ = single crochet (sc)

X̃ = reverse single crochet (rev sc)

◯ = chain (ch)

┼ = double crochet (dc)

SIXTH MOTIF

#6

#7

#5

#8

#4

#9

#3

#2

#1

NECK BAND

1

3

2

4

#9

#8

#7

#1

#6

JOIN HERE TO BEGIN BODY RND 1

#3

#5

#4

FIRST MOTIF

#1

#9

#2

#8

#2

#3

#7

#4

#5

#6

SECOND MOTIF

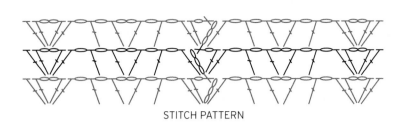

STITCH PATTERN

ch-1 sp, ch 1] 4 times, make 15 dc over the ch-9 sp, hdc in the next ch-1 sp of the center, turn.

ARMS 3–8 Make in the same way as Arm 2.

ARM 9 AND CONNECT TO ARM 1 Make in the same way as Arm 2, except omit the last hdc, instead sl st in the 2nd ch of the beginning ch of Arm 1 (which may be hidden under the last of 13 dc), turn.

TO COMPLETE ARM 1 Sl st in each of the next 7 dc, ch 3, sl st in the marked 4th ch at the tip of Arm 1, [ch 1, skip the next dc, dc in the next dc] 4 times, turn. Ch 4, [dc in the next ch-1 sp, ch 1] 4 times, end with sl st in the top of the next ch-3 (the beginning ch of Arm 1), fasten off.

—To join motifs at ch-4 sp at the tip of arm:

JOIN Instead of ch 4 at the tip of the arm, make ch 3, sl st in the ch-4 sp at the tip of the corresponding arm of the previous motif, ch 1, continue on the working motif.

INSTRUCTIONS
Motif Yoke

The top begins with 6 motifs joined as you go into a ring that forms the yoke. Motifs are connected to each other at two arms on either side. The two uppermost arms (first and ninth) will be connected for the neckline; the three lowermost arms (fourth, fifth, and sixth) will be connected for the body.

First Motif

Make the basic motif complete, without joins, mark as the First Motif.

Second Motif

Make the basic motif through Arm 6, join the tip of Arm 7 to the tip of previous motif Arm 3; join the tip of Arm 8 to the tip of previous motif Arm 2; complete the motif.

Third to Fifth Motifs

Make and join in the same way as the Second Motif.

Sixth Motif

Make Arm 1, join the tip of Arm 2 to the tip of First Motif Arm 8; join the tip of Arm 3 to the tip of First Motif Arm 7; complete Arms 4–6; join the tip of Arm 7 to the tip of Fifth Motif Arm 3; join the tip of Arm 8 to the tip of Fifth Motif Arm 2; complete the motif.

Neckband

Twelve arms of motifs are free at the neck opening. With RS of the yoke ring facing, begin in the Sixth Motif at the top of one shoulder, connect 12 arms and make the neckband with RS always facing.

RND 1 Join yarn with sl st in the ch-4 sp at the tip of Sixth Motif Arm 1, ch 1, insert hook in the same ch-4 sp, YO and draw up a loop, insert hook in the ch-4 sp at the tip of marked First Motif Arm 9, YO and draw up a loop (3 loops on hook), YO and draw through all 3 loops on hook to sc2tog at the first shoulder; *ch 8, sc in the next ch-4 tip, ch 2, trtr in the next join between motifs, ch 2, trtr in the same join, ch 2, sc in the next ch-4 tip*; repeat from * to * once, ch 8, sc2tog in the next 2 ch-4 tips at the other shoulder; repeat from * to * twice, ch 8, end with sl st in the beginning sc.

RND 2 Ch 1, sc in the same sc, *[8 sc in the next ch-8 sp, sc in the next sc, 2 sc in the next ch-2 sp, sc in the next trtr, 2 sc in the next ch-2 sp, sc in the next trtr, 2 sc in the next ch-2 sp, sc in the next sc] twice, 8 sc in the next ch-8 sp, sc in the next sc at the shoulder*; repeat from * to * once, except omit the last sc, instead end with sl st in the beginning sc—90 sc.

RND 3 Ch 4 (counts as dc, ch 1), skip the first sc, [skip the next sc, dc in the next sc, ch 1] 44 times around, end with sl st in the 3rd ch of the beginning ch—45 dc.

RND 4 Ch 1, moving in the reverse direction, rev sc in the first ch-1 sp, ch 1, [rev sc in the next ch-1 sp, ch 1] 44 times, end with sl st in the same ch-1 sp as at the beginning, fasten off.

Body

Eighteen arms of motifs are free at the body opening. With RS facing, locate marked First Motif, join with sl st in the ch-4 tip at Arm 6; begin working in the free arms of the same motif, moving across what will be the armhole.

RND 1 (RS) Ch 11 (counts as dc, ch 8), *trtr in the next join between motifs, ch 3, trtr in the same join, ch 8, [dc, ch 3, dc] in ch-4 tip of the next arm, ch 8, [sc, ch 3, sc] in the ch-4 sp tip of the next arm (center of motif), ch 8**, [dc, ch 3, dc] in the ch-4 tip of the next arm, ch 8*; repeat from * to * 4 times; repeat from * ending at **; dc in the same ch-4 tip as at the beginning, ch 1, hdc in the 3rd ch of the beginning ch.

RND 2 (RS) Ch 3 (counts as dc), dc in the first ch-sp, [9 dc in the next ch-8 sp, SH in the next ch-3 sp] 23 times around, 9 dc in the last ch-8 sp, end with 2 dc in the same ch-sp as at the beginning, ch 1, sc in the 3rd ch of the beginning ch, turn—24 shells.

RND 3 (WS) Ch 3, dc in the first ch-sp, *ch 1, skip the remaining 2 dc of the shell, skip the next dc, dc in the next dc, ch 1, skip the next 2 dc, V in the next dc, ch 1, skip the next 2 dc, dc in the next dc, ch 1, SH in the next shell*; repeat from * to * 23 times, except omit the last SH, instead end with 2 dc in the same ch-sp as at the beginning, ch 1, sc in the 3rd ch of the beginning ch, turn.

RNDS 4–6 Work Patt Rnd for 3 rounds.

Fit Tip

For a deeper or higher armhole, add or omit rounds here, end by working a right-side round.

Join the front and back Body at the underarms, making one continuous round by adding stitches at each underarm. The next round begins by working in stitch pattern across the Body.

RND 7 (JOIN UNDERARMS) Begin as Patt Rnd, *work in stitch pattern as established, completing 6 shells across the body, ch 1, Fsc 9 for the underarm, skip the next 5 shells for the sleeve, SH in the next shell*; repeat from * to * once, except omit the last SH, instead end with 2 dc in the same sp as at the beginning, ch 1, sc in the 3rd ch of the beginning ch, turn.

RND 8 Ch 3, dc in the first ch-sp, *ch 1, skip the first sc of the underarm foundation, dc in the next sc, ch 1, skip the next 2 sc, V in the next sc, ch 1, skip the next 2 sc, dc in the next sc, ch 1, skip the remaining sc*, SH in the next shell, work in stitch pattern as established*, ending with SH in the shell before the other underarm foundation; repeat from * to * once, end with 2 dc in the same ch-sp as at the beginning, ch 1, sc in the 3rd ch of the beginning ch, turn—14 shells.

RNDS 9–17 Work Patt Rnd for 9 rounds.

Fit Tip

For a longer or shorter top, add or omit rounds here as desired, end by working a wrong-side round.

Scallop Trim

RND 18 (RS) Ch 3, 2 dc in the first ch-sp, (3 dc, ch 3, 3 dc) in the ch-2 sp of the next V, [(3 dc, ch 3, 3 dc) in the ch-2 sp of the next shell, (3 dc, ch 3, 3 dc) in the next V] 13 times, end with 3 dc in the same ch-sp as at the beginning, ch 3, sl st in the 3rd ch of the beginning ch, fasten off.

Sleeves

With WS facing, at one underarm, skip the chains of the foundation, skip the next dc row edge, join with sl st in the next ch-2 sp of the shell (the same sp as previously worked with SH during the Rnd 7 underarm joining).

RND 1 (WS) Ch 3, dc in the first ch-sp, work in stitch pattern as established around the sleeve to other side of the underarm through 6 shells, placing the last SH in the ch-2 sp of the shell before underarm (the same sp as previously worked with SH), ch 1, skip the first ch of the underarm foundation, dc in the next ch, ch 1, skip the next 2 ch, V in the next ch, ch 1, skip the next 2 ch, dc in the next ch, ch 1, skip the remaining ch, end with 2 dc in the same ch-sp as at the beginning, ch 1, sc in the 3rd ch of the beginning ch, turn—7 shells.

RNDS 2–13 Work Patt Rnd for 12 rounds.

Fit Tip

For longer or shorter sleeves, add or omit rounds here as desired. End by working a wrong-side round.

Scallop Trim

RND 14 (RS) Make Scallop Trim around the sleeve in the same way as Body Rnd 18, fasten off.

Make sleeve and trim around the other armhole in the same way.

Weave in ends, block top.

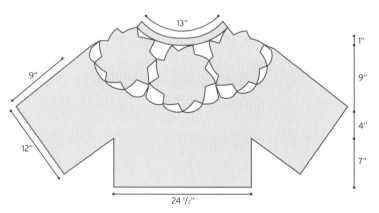

RIVER SONG SKIRT

—— •• ✦ •• ——

THE INSPIRATION FOR THIS DESIGN IS AN EIGHT-POINTED ROUND DOILY, WHICH I SERIOUSLY MESSED WITH AND ADAPTED TO HAVE FIVE, SIX, AND SEVEN POINTS. ALTHOUGH EACH SHIFT MAKES THE MOTIFS PROGRESSIVELY LARGER, THE DISTANCE ALONG THE SIDES FROM POINT TO POINT REMAINS CONSTANT. MY EIGHTH-GRADE GEOMETRY TEACHER, MRS. COHEN, WOULD HAVE BEEN ASTOUNDED, CONSIDERING THAT HERS WAS NEVER MY BEST SUBJECT. BY CLEVERLY FITTING THE EQUAL SIDES TOGETHER, YOU CAN CREATE THE FLARE IN THIS BELOW-THE-KNEE SKIRT.

TO CREATE A NICELY FITTED, SMOOTH YOKE OR TOP PART IN A PULL-ON SKIRT, SKIRT 101 (PAGE 129) IS THE WAY TO GO. FOR RIVER SONG I HAVE ALTERED THE SHELL PATTERN COUNT AND THE FINISHED SIZE RANGE OF THE SKIRT 101 TEMPLATE TO PRESENT SHELLS IN A MULTIPLE OF THREE. THAT'S THE MAGIC NUMBER FOR ADDING THIS BRILLIANT ARRAY OF MOTIFS.

SKILL LEVEL: INTERMEDIATE ✦ ✦ ✦ ✦

SIZE
XS/S (M, L, XL/2XL, 3XL); finished high hip 36 (40, 45, 49, 54)" (91 [101.5, 114, 124.5, 137]cm); sample shown is XS with no-sew elastic waist

MATERIALS
Tahki Cotton Classic; 100% mercerized cotton; 1.75 oz (50g)/108 yd (100m) per hank (DK weight) ③

—7 (8, 9, 10, 11) hanks in #3715 Spring Green

Size I-9 (5.5mm) crochet hook

Split-ring stitch markers or scraps of yarn for markers

Blunt yarn needle

For no-sew elastic waist, ⅛" (3mm) narrow braided or round elastic, cut to measure

GAUGE (AS CROCHETED)
11 Fsc or sc = 4" (10cm)

In Basic Shell Stitch Pattern, (shell, sc) 2 times = 3" (7.5cm); 4 rounds = 2¼" (5.5cm) (will lengthen with blocking to 4 rounds = 2½" [6.5cm] or more)

Five-point motif, 6" (15cm) at widest/tallest

Six-point motif, 7" (18cm) at widest/tallest

Seven-point motif, 8" (20.5cm) at widest/tallest

For all motifs, 4" (10cm) along one side from point to the next point

STITCHES USED
Fsc (see page 134 for technique), sl st, ch, sc, dc

STITCH DEFINITIONS
SH (SHELL) (dc, ch 1, dc, ch 1, dc) all in the same stitch or space.

INC-SH (INCREASE SHELL) (dc, ch 1, dc, ch 1, dc, ch 1, dc) all in the same stitch or space.

For Basic Shell Stitch Pattern (in rounds), see Skirt 101 (page 129) and explanations in Jacket 101 (page 120).

BASIC MOTIFS
Motifs are crocheted and assembled with RS always facing. They are joined as you go while making the last round. To keep this project portable for as long as possible, you can make all the motifs complete, but leave extra-long tails before cutting the yarn. When you want to assemble the skirt, rip out as much of each motif as you need, then recrochet, joining as you go.

Five-Point Motif

RND 1 Ch 5, sl st in the beginning ch to form a ring, ch 5 (counts as a dc, ch 2), [dc, ch 2] 9 times in the ring, end with sl st in the 3rd ch of the beginning ch—10 dc.

RND 2 Ch 3 (counts as dc), dc in the first dc, *ch 2, skip the next ch-2 sp, dc in the next dc, ch 2, skip the next ch-2 sp, [2 dc, ch 2, 2 dc] for a point in the next dc*; repeat from * to * 4 times, except omit the last (2 dc, ch 2, 2 dc), instead end with 2 dc in the same dc as at the beginning, ch 1, sc in the 3rd ch of the beginning ch—5 points.

RND 3 Ch 3, 2 dc in the first sp, *ch 3, skip the next ch-2 sp, dc in the next dc, ch 3, skip the next ch-2 sp, [3 dc, ch 2, 3 dc] in ch-2 sp of the next point*; repeat from * to * 4 times, except omit the last (3 dc, ch 2, 3 dc), instead end with 3 dc in the same sp as at the beginning, ch 1, sc in the 3rd ch of the beginning ch.

RND 4 Ch 3, 3 dc in the first sp, *ch 3, skip the next ch-3 sp, dc in the next dc, ch 3, skip the next ch-3 sp, [4 dc, ch 2, 4 dc] in ch-2 sp of the next point*; repeat from * to * 4 times, except omit the last (4 dc, ch 2, 4 dc), instead end with 4 dc in the same sp as at the beginning, ch 2, sl st in the 3rd ch of the beginning ch.

Six-Point Motif

RND 1 Ch 5, sl st in the beginning ch to form a ring, ch 1, 12 sc in the ring, sl st in the beginning sc—12 sc.

RND 2 Ch 5 (counts dc, ch 2), skip the first sc, [dc in the next sc, ch 2] 11 times, end with sl st in the 3rd ch of the beginning ch—12 dc.

RND 3 Same as Five-Point Motif Rnd 2 for 6 points.

RND 4 Same as Five-Point Motif Rnd 3 for 6 points.

RND 5 Same as Five-Point Motif Rnd 4 for 6 points.

Seven-Point Motif

RND 1 Ch 5, sl st in the beg ch to form a ring, ch 3 (counts as dc), 13 dc in the ring, sl st in the 3rd ch of the beginning ch—14 dc.

RND 2 Ch 5 (counts as dc, ch 2), skip the first dc, [dc in the next dc, ch 2] 13 times, end with sl st in the 3rd ch of the beginning ch—14 dc.

RND 3 Same as Five-Point Motif Rnd 2 for 7 points.

RND 4 Same as Five-Point Motif Rnd 3 for 7 points.

RND 5 Same as Five-Point Motif Rnd 4 for 7 points.

—To connect motifs to each other at a point:

POINT JOIN On the working motif, make the first 4 dc in the ch-2 sp of the next point, sl st in the ch-2 sp of the corresponding point of the previous motif, make 4 dc in the same sp of the working motif.

—To connect motifs to each other at the middle of a side:

SIDE JOIN After completing a point, ch 3, dc in the next dc in the middle of a side, sl st in the corresponding dc of the previous motif, ch 3, continue on the working motif.

—To connect a Five-Point Motif at the ch-3 sp of a side to 2 shells of the yoke:

CH JOIN After completing a point on the working motif, ch 1, sl st in the 2nd dc of the next shell of the yoke, ch 1, skip the next ch-3 sp of the motif, dc in the next dc, ch 1, sl st in the 2nd dc of the next shell of the yoke, ch 1, continue on the working motif.

—To join motifs at a point where there is already a join, make the sl st by inserting hook into the previous sl st at the join, under 2 strands. The exception is when motifs are joined to the yoke; make the sl st into the same dc as the previous join.

INSTRUCTIONS
Skirt Yoke

The skirt starts at the center back with a yoke made in the same way as the Skirt 101 yoke (page 131), but with different sizing. Sizes M and XL/2XL contain one extra odd shell, which will be added to the count at the back for hip-shaping purposes.

Fsc 80 (92, 104, 116, 128), turn foundation so the sc edge is on top, sl st in the beginning sc to form a ring, being careful not to twist the foundation, begin work across the sc edge.

Following the instructions for Skirt 101 (page 129), make a basic skirt body with these changes:

Size XS/S

RNDS 1–8 Make in the same way as Skirt 101 Size XS, with hip shaping, Rnds 1–8, fasten off—24 shells.

Size M

RNDS 1–5 Make in the same way as Skirt 101 Size S Rnds 1–5 for 23 shell repeats instead of 22, end by working a Patt M, with a sc now at the center back.

RND 6 Ch 3, *[sc in the 2nd dc of the next shell, SH in the next sc] twice, sc in the 2nd dc of the next shell, INC-SH in the next sc, [sc in the 2nd dc of the next shell, SH in the next sc] 5 times, sc in the 2nd dc of the next shell, INC-SH in the next sc, [sc in the 2nd dc of the next shell, SH in the next sc] twice*; repeat from * to * once, sc in the 2nd dc of the next shell, (dc, ch 1, dc) in the same sc as at the beginning, sc in the 3rd ch of the beginning ch, turn—23 shells.

RND 7 Begin as Patt M; work even across increase points as Patt H; end as Patt M—27 shells.

RND 8 Work as Patt N, fasten off.

Size L

RNDS 1–5 Make in the same way as Skirt 101 Size L, Rnds 1–5, end by working a Patt M—26 shells.

RNDS 6-7 Make in the same way as Skirt 101 Size L, hip shaping, Rnds 8–9—30 shells.

RND 8 Work as Patt N, fasten off.

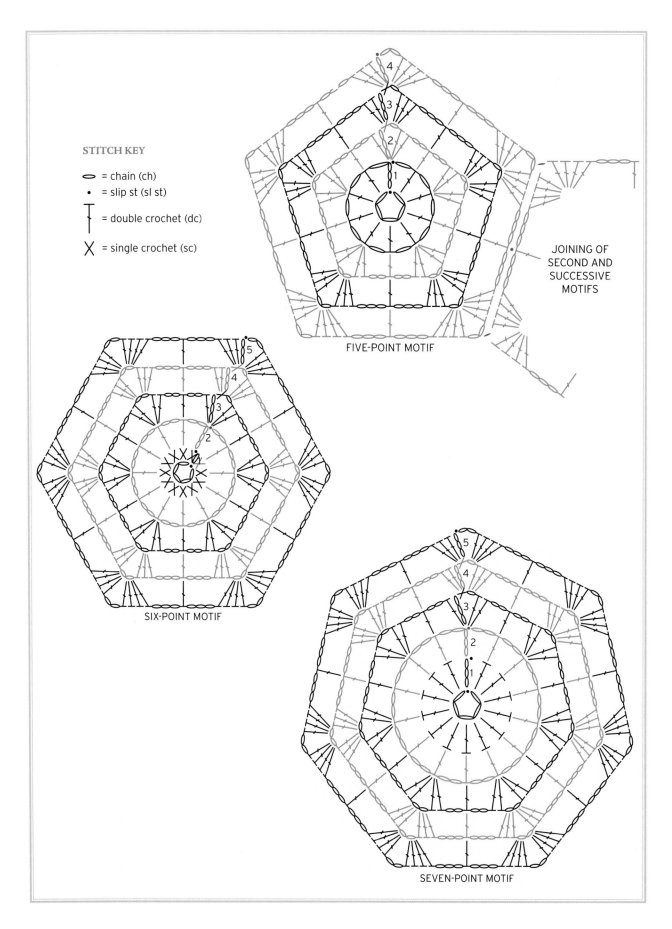

STITCH KEY

⬭ = chain (ch)

• = slip st (sl st)

T = double crochet (dc)

X = single crochet (sc)

JOINING OF
SECOND AND
SUCCESSIVE
MOTIFS

FIVE-POINT MOTIF

SIX-POINT MOTIF

SEVEN-POINT MOTIF

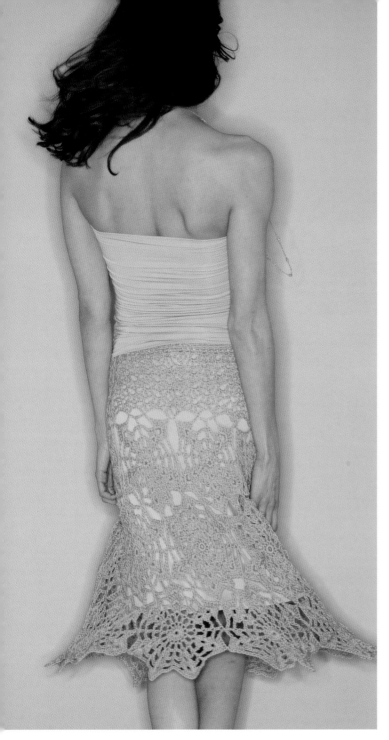

RND 10 Begin as Patt N; work even across increase points as Patt H, end as Patt N, fasten off—33 shells

Size 3XL
RNDS 1–10 Make in the same way as Skirt 101 Size 3XL, with hip shaping, Rnds 1–10, fasten off—36 shells.

Fit Tip
For a longer skirt, add rounds here before attaching the motif body, working [Patt M, Patt N] for length desired, end by working a Patt N.

Motif Body
All Sizes
The last round of the skirt is now RS, with a shell at the center back and 24 (27, 30, 33, 36) shells, a multiple of three. Continue with RS of the skirt facing. The Skirt Body consists of three tiers of 8 (9, 10, 11, 12) motifs in each tier, following assembly diagram below. Five-Point Motifs of Tier 1 are joined as you go to each other and to three shells of the skirt, starting at the center back. Six-Point Motifs of Tier 2 are joined as you go to each other and to Tier 1. Seven-Point Motifs of Tier 3 are joined as you go to each other and to Tier 2.

Tier 1
MOTIF 1 Make a Five-Point Motif through 3 sides, at the next point, Point Join to the 2nd dc of the center back shell, Ch Join to the 2nd dc of each of the next 2 shells of the skirt, Point Join to the 2nd dc of the next shell of the skirt, complete the motif, fasten off.

MOTIF 2 Make a Five-Point Motif through 3 sides, at the next point, Point Join to the corresponding point of the previous motif, Side Join to the previous motif, Point Join to the same dc of the shell of the skirt as the previous motif, Ch Join to the 2nd dc of each of the next 2 shells of the skirt, Point Join to the 2nd dc of the next shell of the skirt, except omit the last 4 dc, instead end with sl st in the 3rd ch of the beginning ch, fasten off.

MOTIFS 3–7 (8, 9, 10, 11) Assemble in the same way as Motif 2.

LAST MOTIF Make a Five-Point Motif through 2 sides, at the next point, Point Join to the corresponding point of the previous motif, Side Join to the previous motif, Point Join to the same dc of the shell of the skirt as the previous motif, Ch Join to the 2nd dc of each of the next 2 shells of the skirt, Point Join to the same dc of the shell of the skirt as Motif 1, Side Join to Motif 1, Point Join to Motif 1, except omit the last 4 dc, instead end with sl st in the 3rd ch of the beginning ch, fasten off.

Size XL/2XL
RNDS 1–7 Make in the same way as Skirt 101 Size XL, Rnds 1–7, for 29 shell repeats instead of 28.

RND 8 Repeat as Patt N once more.

RND 9 Ch 1, sc in the next dc, *[SH in the next sc, sc in the 2nd dc of the next shell] 3 times, INC-SH in the next sc, sc in the 2nd dc of the next shell; [SH in the next sc, sc in the 2nd dc of the next shell] 7 times, INC-SH in the next sc, sc in the 2nd dc of the next shell; [SH in the next sc, sc in the 2nd dc of the next shell] twice*; repeat from * to * once, end with SH in the next sc, sl st in the beginning sc, turn.

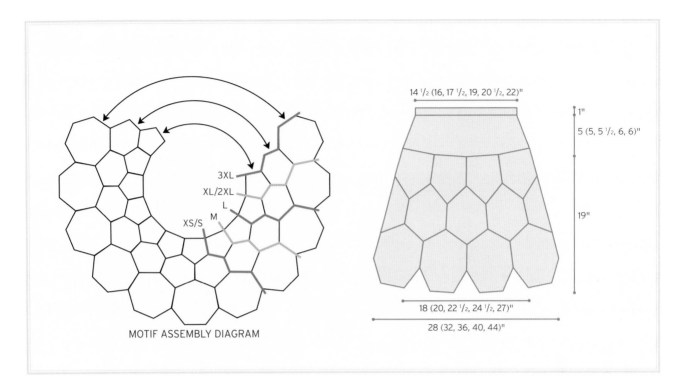

14 1/2 (16, 17 1/2, 19, 20 1/2, 22)"

1"

5 (5, 5 1/2, 6, 6)"

19"

18 (20, 22 1/2, 24 1/2, 27)"

28 (32, 36, 40, 44)"

3XL
XL/2XL
L
M
XS/S

MOTIF ASSEMBLY DIAGRAM

Tier 2

MOTIF 1 Make a Six-Point Motif through 3 sides, at the next point, Point Join to the unworked point at the bottom of any motif of Tier 1, Side Join to the same motif, Point Join to the next Point Join of Tier 1, Side Join to the next motif of Tier 1, Point Join to the next point of the same motif, complete the motif, fasten off.

MOTIF 2 Make a Six-Point Motif through 3 sides, at the next point, Point Join to the corresponding point of the previous motif, Side Join to the same motif, Point Join to the next point join, Side Join to the next motif of Tier 1, Point Join to the next Point Join of Tier 1, Side Join to the next motif of Tier 1, Point Join to the next point of the same motif of Tier 1, except omit the last 4 dc, instead end with sl st in the 3rd ch of the beginning ch, fasten off.

MOTIFS 3–7 (8, 9, 10, 11) Assemble in the same way as Motif 2.

LAST MOTIF Make a Six-Point Motif through 2 sides, at the next point, Point Join to the corresponding point of the previous motif, Side Join to the same motif, Point Join to the next Point Join, Side Join to the next motif of Tier 1, Point Join to the next Point Join of Tier 1, Side Join to the next motif of Tier 1, Point Join to the next Point Join of the same motif, Side Join to Motif 1, Point Join to Motif 1, except omit the last 4 dc, instead end with sl st in the 3rd ch of the beginning ch, fasten off.

Tier 3

MOTIF 1 Make a Seven-Point Motif through 4 sides, at the next point, Point Join to the unworked point at the bottom of any motif of Tier 2, Side Join to the same motif, Point Join to the next Point Join of Tier 2, Side Join to the next motif of Tier 2, Point Join to the next point of the same motif, complete the motif, fasten off.

MOTIF 2 Make a Seven-Point Motif through 4 sides, at the next point, Point Join to the corresponding point of the previous motif, Side Join to the same motif, Point Join to the next Point Join, Side Join to the next motif of Tier 2, Point Join to the next Point Join of Tier 2, Side Join to the next motif of Tier 2, Point Join to the next point of the same motif of Tier 2, except omit the last 4 dc, instead end with sl st in the 3rd ch of the beginning ch, fasten off.

MOTIFS 3–7 (8, 9, 10, 11) Assemble in the same way as Motif 2.

LAST MOTIF Make a Seven-Point Motif through 3 sides, at the next point, Point Join to the corresponding point of the previous motif, Side Join to the same motif, Point Join to the next Point Join, Side Join to the next motif of Tier 2, Point Join to the next Point Join of Tier 2, Side Join to the next motif of Tier 2, Point Join to the next Point Join of the same motif, Side Join to Motif 1, Point Join to Motif 1, except omit the last 4 dc, instead end with sl st in the 3rd ch of the beginning ch, fasten off.

Waistband

Refer to Skirt 101 (page 129) for drawstring or elastic waist options. Make the waistband desired in the same way, using 80 (92, 104, 116, 128) stitches of the foundation chain.

Weave in ends, block skirt.

Exploded Doily Lace

Round and Round

BY DOILY I REFER TO THE TRADITIONAL FORM: ONE PIECE, crocheted from the center outwards, generally in open or lace stitches. It is the way in which each doily pattern solves the challenge of growing from a center point to its full outer circumference that makes doilies so special to me. I am fascinated by the progression of increases that must, by the laws of geometry, radiate out from the center. I analyze and obsess over why and when they are applied, and how they are handled. The great doilies are stories in crochet, with a beginning, character development, and plot twists, periods of conflict, growth and redemption. And the best of them have slam-bang endings.

There isn't a whole heck of a lot you can do with an exploded intact doily. It's the same flat lace thing, only bigger. However, when you start deconstructing the lace pattern, accelerating or retarding the growth rate of the rounds, perhaps scooping out the middle bits, the real fun begins.

FELINA SKIRT

I AM NOT A GREAT DANCER, BUT AN AVID ONE. THERE ARE MUSIC TRACKS THAT COMPEL ME TO GET UP AND GROOVE, OFTEN TO THE DISMAY OF THE OTHER SHOPPERS AT THE SUPERMARKET. WELL, I CAN'T BE BLAMED IF THEY'RE PIPING IN COOL TUNES, CAN I? CERTAIN ARTICLES OF CLOTHING DO THE SAME THING FOR ME. PUT ME IN A SWINGY FULL SKIRT AND I'M A TWIRLING FOOL. THAT KIND OF EXPLAINS WHY I DON'T DARE WEAR SKIRTS TO THE SUPERMARKET.

ENGINEERING AN EXPLODED ROUND DOILY INTO A WEARABLE SKIRT TAKES INTUITION AS WELL AS CALCULATION. THE MOST SUCCESSFUL TRANSFORMATIONS HAPPEN WHEN THE ORIGINAL DOILY PRESENTS THE RIGHT PROPORTIONS OF CENTER ROUNDS TO OUTER ROUNDS AS WELL AS A CLEAR AND LOGICAL PLACE TO START REMOVING THE UNWANTED PARTS. THEN IT IS A SIMPLE MATTER OF SKIPPING THE CENTER ROUNDS, INSTEAD BEGINNING THE OUTER ROUNDS ON A FOUNDATION RING.

A FULL CIRCLE SKIRT IS HARD TO WEAR FOR MOST FIGURES. IT PLACES TOO MUCH FABRIC TOO SOON AROUND THE HIPS. I'VE ADJUSTED THE GROWTH RATE OF THE LACE SECTIONS IN THE DOILY TO DELAY THE BIGGEST FLARE UNTIL MID-THIGH. FELINA IS NICELY BALANCED AND LONG ENOUGH TO SWIRL AROUND YOUR KNEES.

SKILL LEVEL: EASY ✦ ✦ ✦ ✦

SIZE
S (M, L, XL, 2XL); finished full hip 9" (23cm) below waist 56 (64, 72, 80, 88)" (142 [163, 183, 203, 223.5]cm); finished length: 21" (53.5cm); sample shown is size S with drawstring waist

MATERIALS
Tahki Cotton Classic; 100% mercerized cotton; 1.75 oz (50g)/108 yd (100m) per hank (3)

—6 (7, 8, 9, 10) hanks in #3003 Natural

Size H-8 (5mm) crochet hook

GAUGE (AS CROCHETED)
12 Fsc or sc = 4" (10cm)

In lace pattern, 3 Vs = 3" (7.5cm); 3 rows Vs = 3" (7.5cm) (will lengthen with blocking to 3 rows = 3½" [9cm], with lace scallops hanging even longer)

STITCHES USED
Fsc (see page 134 for technique), sl st, ch, sc, tr, rev sc

STITCH DEFINITIONS
CL (TR2TOG CLUSTER) YO twice, insert hook in the next stitch or space, YO and draw up a loop (4 loops on hook), [YO and draw through 2 loops on hook] twice (2 loops left on hook), YO twice, insert hook in the same stitch or space, YO and draw up a loop (5 loops on hook), [YO and draw through 2 loops on hook] twice (3 loops left on hook), YO and draw through all 3 loops.

BEG-CL (BEGINNING CLUSTER) Ch 3, tr in the beginning sp formed by hdc.

V [CL, ch 3, CL] in the same stitch or space.

V IN V V in ch-3 sp of the next V.

STITCH KEY

$\Join$ = foundation sc (fsc)

• = slip st (sl st)

= Beg-CL

= V (CL, ch 3, CL)

= tr2tog cluster (CL)

= chain (ch)

$\top$ = half double crochet (hdc)

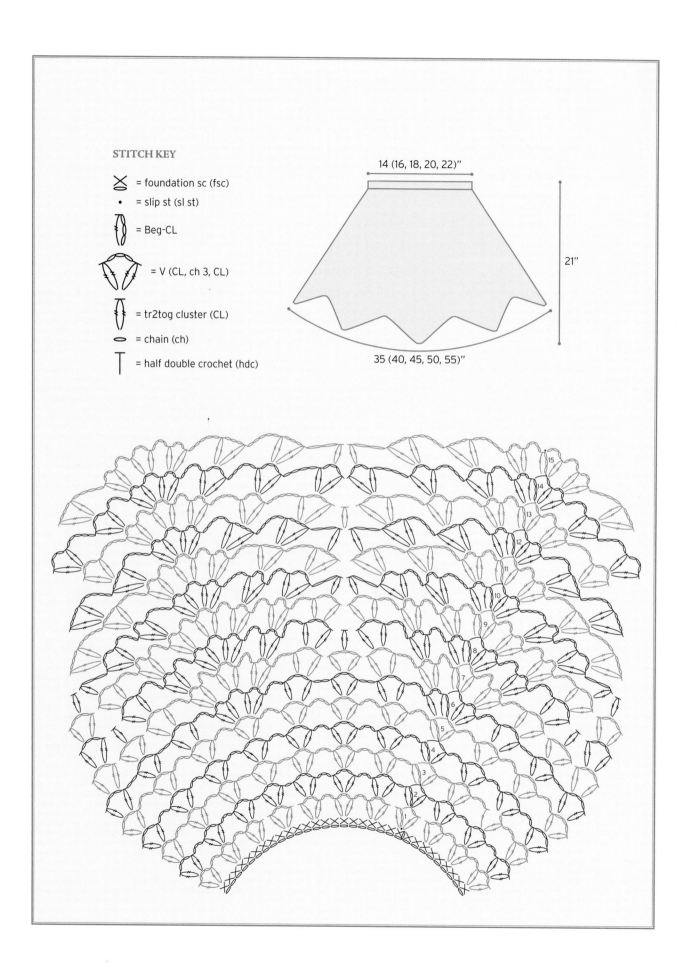

14 (16, 18, 20, 22)"

21"

35 (40, 45, 50, 55)"

INSTRUCTIONS

The skirt is crocheted from the top down in joined rounds with RS always facing.

Fsc 84 (96, 108, 120, 132), turn the foundation so the sc edge is on top, sl st in the beginning sc to form a ring, careful not to twist the foundation, begin work across the sc edge.

RND 1 Ch 3, tr in the same first sc, *skip the next 2 sc, V in the next sc, skip the next 2 sc, (ch 3, V, ch 3) in the next sc, [skip the next 2 sc, V in the next sc] twice*; repeat from * to * 6 (7, 8, 9, 10) times, except omit the last V, instead end with CL in the same sc as at the beginning, ch 1, hdc in the 3rd ch of the beginning ch—28 (32, 36, 40, 44) Vs to make 7 (8, 9, 10, 11) lace repeats.

RND 2 Beg-CL, ch 1, *V in the next V, ch 3, V in the next V, ch 3, [V in the next V, ch 1] twice*; repeat from * to * 6 (7, 8, 9, 10) times, except omit the last V and ch 1, instead end with CL in the same sp as at the beginning, ch 1, hdc in the 3rd ch of the beginning ch.

RND 3 Beg-CL, ch 2, *V in the next V, ch 3, V in the next V, ch 3, [V in the next V, ch 2] twice*; repeat from * to * around, except omit the last V and ch 2, instead end with CL in the same sp as at the beginning, ch 1, hdc in the 3rd ch of the beginning ch.

RND 4 Beg-CL, [ch 3, V in the next V] around, end with CL in the same sp as at the beginning, ch 1, hdc in the 3rd ch of the beginning ch.

RND 5 Beg-CL, [ch 4, V in the next V] around, end with CL in the same sp as at the beginning, ch 1, hdc in the 3rd ch of the beginning ch.

RND 6 Beg-CL, ch 3, CL in the same beginning sp, *ch 5, V in the next V, [ch 2, V in the next V] twice, ch 5, (V, ch 3, V) in the next V*; repeat from * to * around, except omit the last ch 3 and V, end with V in the same sp as at the beginning, ch 1, hdc in the 3rd ch of the beginning ch.

RND 7 Beg-CL, *ch 4, V in the next V, ch 5, V in each of the next 3 Vs, ch 5, V in the next V, ch 4, V in the next ch-3 sp between Vs*; repeat from * to * around, except omit the last V, instead end with CL in the same sp as at the beginning, ch 1, hdc in 3rd ch of the beginning ch.

RND 8 Beg-CL, ch 3, CL in the same beginning sp, *[ch 5, V in the next V] twice, CL in ch-3 sp of the next V, [V in the next V, ch 5] twice, (V, ch 3, V) in the next V*; repeat from * to * around, except omit the last ch 3 and V, end with V in the same sp as at the beginning, ch 1, hdc in the 3rd ch of the beginning ch.

RND 9 Beg-CL, *ch 4, V in the next V, ch 5, V in the next V, ch 4, V in the next V, skip the cluster between Vs, V in the next V, ch 4, V in the next V, ch 5, V in the next V, ch 4, V in the next ch-3 sp between Vs*; repeat from * to * around, except omit the last V, instead end with CL in the same sp as at the beginning, ch 1, hdc in the 3rd ch of the beginning ch.

RND 10 Beg-CL, ch 3, CL in the same beginning sp, *[ch 5, V in the next V] twice, ch 2, [CL in ch-3 sp of the next V] twice, ch 2, [V in the next V, ch 5] twice, (V, ch 3, V) in the next V*; repeat from * to * around, except omit the last ch 3 and V, end with V in the same sp as at the beginning, ch 1, hdc in the 3rd ch of the beginning ch.

RND 11 Beg-CL, *ch 4, V in the next V, ch 5, V in the next V, ch 4, V in the next V, skip the next (ch 2, 2 clusters, ch 2), V in the next V, ch 4, V in the next V, ch 5, V in the next V, ch 4, V in the next ch-3 sp between Vs*; repeat from * to * around, except omit the last V, instead end with CL in the same sp as at the beginning, ch 1, hdc in the 3rd ch of the beginning ch.

RND 12 Repeat Rnd 10.

RND 13 Beg-CL, *ch 4, [V in the next V, ch 5] twice, V in the next V, skip the next ch-2 sp, CL in the space between the next 2 clusters, [V in the next V, ch 5] twice, V in the next V, ch 4, V in the next ch-3 sp between Vs*; repeat from * to * around, except omit the last V, instead end with CL in the same sp as at the beginning, ch 1, hdc in the 3rd ch of the beginning ch.

RND 14 Beg-CL, ch 3, CL in the same beginning sp, *[ch 5, V in the next V] twice, ch 4, V in the next V, skip the cluster between Vs, V in the next V, ch 4, [V in the next V, ch 5] twice, (V, ch 3, V) in the next V*; repeat from * to * around, except omit the last ch 3 and V, end with V in the same sp as at the beginning, ch 1, hdc in the 3rd ch of the beginning ch.

RND 15 Beg-CL, *ch 4, [V in the next V, ch 5] twice, V in the next V, ch 2, [CL in ch-3 sp of the next V] twice, ch 2, [V in the next V, ch 5] twice, V in the next V, ch 4, V in the next ch-3 sp between Vs*; repeat from * to * around, except omit the last V, instead end with CL in the same sp as at the beginning, ch 3, sl st in the 3rd ch of the beginning ch, fasten off.

Waistband

Refer to Skirt 101 (page 129) for drawstring or elastic waist options. Make the waistband desired in the same way, using 84 (96, 108, 120, 132) stitches of the foundation chain.

Weave in ends, block skirt.

TOSHIKO POPOVER

— ⋅⋅ ◆ ⋅⋅ —

IT WAS A FRIEND, DEE STANZIANO, WHO TRANSFORMED ONE OF MY CAPELET PATTERNS INTO A TWIRLY DANCE SKIRT FOR HER DAUGHTER. NOW I'M DOING JUST THE OPPOSITE. USING THE SAME ROUNDS OF LACE PATTERN AS THE PREVIOUS FELINA SKIRT AND SWAPPING OUT FOR A COZY SOFT WORSTED-WEIGHT WOOL-BLEND YARN IN AN EVEN MORE EXPLODED GAUGE, YOU CAN MAKE THIS ROOMY, LIGHTWEIGHT POPOVER TO USE IN LAYERING INSTEAD OF A JACKET OR SWEATER. FINISH THE TOP EDGE WITH DEEP RIBBING RATHER THAN THE SKIRT WAISTBAND AND YOU HAVE A SWEET EXTENDED COWL NECK THAT YOU CAN ARRANGE LIKE A PORTRAIT COLLAR.

SKILL LEVEL: EASY ◆ ◆ ◆ ◆

SIZE

Average (Plus) to fit most; finished neck 30 (32)" (76 [81]cm); finished full bust 9" (23cm) below foundation 56 (64)" (142 [163]cm); length 22" (56cm); sample is size Average

MATERIALS

NaturallyCaron.com Country; 75% microdenier acrylic, 25% merino wool; 3 oz (85g)/185 yd (170m) (4)

— 4 (5) skeins in #0015 Deep Taupe

Size J-10 (6mm) crochet hook

Size I-9 (5.5mm) crochet hook, for collar ribbing

Blunt yarn needle

GAUGE (AS CROCHETED)

11 Fsc = 4" (10cm)

In lace pattern, 3 Vs = 3½" (9cm); 3 rows Vs = 4" (10cm) (will lengthen with blocking to 3 rows = 4½" (11.5cm), with lace scallops hanging even longer)

In sctbl ribbing, using the smaller hook, 15 sts = 4", 12 rows = 4"

STITCHES USED

Fsc (see page 134 for technique), sl st, ch, sc, sctbl, tr

For doily lace stitch definitions and lace pattern rounds, see Felina Skirt (page 89).

INSTRUCTIONS

The popover is crocheted from the top down in joined rounds with RS always facing.

With the larger hook, Fsc 84 (96), turn the foundation so the sc edge is on top, sl st in the beginning sc to form a ring, careful not to twist foundation, begin work across the sc edge.

RNDS 1–15 For Toshiko sizes Average (Plus), make in the same way as Felina Skirt (page 89) Rnds 1–15 for sizes S (M), fasten off.

> *Fit Tip*
>
> This is a generously open neckline. If your shoulders are narrow or you prefer a smaller opening, work the next edging round more firmly to gather the neck as desired.

Collar

With RS facing, using the smaller hook, join yarn with sl st in the first st of the foundation chain of the neck.

EDGING RND (RS) Ch 1, sc in each ch of the foundation, sl st in the beginning sc, do not turn—80 (88) sc.

Create stitches for the collar and work sideways in sctbl ribbing, connecting to the neckline as you go.

ROW 1 (RS) Ch 1, insert hook in the same sc, Fsc 23, turn.

ROW 2 (WS) Working across the sc edge of the foundation, ch 1, sctbl in each of the next 23 sc, sl st in each of the next 2 ch of the neck, turn.

ROW 3 Do not chain, skip loops of 2 sl sts, sctbl in each of the next 23 sc, turn.

ROW 4 Ch 1, sctbl in each of the next 23 sc, sl st in each of the next 2 ch of neck, turn.

Repeat Rows 3–4 around, ending with sl st in the last ch of the neck, sl st in the same ch as at the beginning, fasten off leaving a 12" (30.5cm) long tail for sewing. Thread the tail onto a blunt yarn needle. With RS facing, match the sc of the last row of ribbing with sts of the foundation. Insert the needle right to left under 2 strands of the first foundation chain, insert needle left to right under the front loop only of the first sc of ribbing; insert the needle right to left under 2 strands of the next foundation chain, insert the needle left to right under the front loop only of the next sc of ribbing, sewing to the end. Avoid pulling up stitches too tightly. Fasten yarn, weave in ends, block. Do not steam or press ribbing.

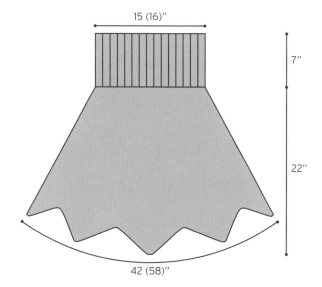

BOZENA DRESS

•————••✦••————•

RARELY DO I DESIGN A GARMENT THAT I CAN'T WEAR, BUT IT HAPPENS. WITH A FEW DAYS TO GO BEFORE I HAD TO LEAVE FOR THE 2008 CGOA NATIONAL CONFERENCE IN NEW HAMPSHIRE, I WAS HAVING A MAJOR ANXIETY ATTACK TRYING TO STYLE THIS BOZENA DRESS IN A VAIN (AS IN VANITY) AND VAIN (AS IN USELESS) ATTEMPT TO MAKE THE THING WORK FOR MY MIDDLE-AGED, PLUM-TOMATO SHAPE. I PACKED THE UNWEARABLE, DESPICABLE RAG ANYWAY, AND ON A WHIM I ASKED MY FRIEND, VASHTI BRAHA, TO TRY IT ON. THE IMMEDIATE EFFECT LITERALLY TOOK MY BREATH AWAY. THERE WASN'T A DAMN THING WRONG WITH THE DRESS. BOZENA SKIMS THE BODY AND HAS NO SHAPE OTHER THAN THE CURVES OF THE WEARER. ON ME, MADE IN A SIZE WITH AN INCH (2.5CM) OF EASE AT THE BUST, IT HANGS LIMPLY. THE SAME SIZE, RESULTING IN AN INCH OF NEGATIVE EASE ON CURVACEOUS VASHTI, WAS HUBBA-HUBBA.

BOZENA TAKES THE DOILY ROUNDS USED IN THE FELINE SKIRT AND SPLICES THEM ONTO A DROPPED-WAIST LACE BODICE. THE NECKLINE IS DEEPLY SCOOPED, EMBRACING THE TOP OF THE SHOULDERS, PERHAPS SLIDING OFF JUST A TAD IF THE MOOD AND OCCASION CALL FOR IT. THE YARN HELPS MAKE THIS A BIG-NIGHT OUTFIT, WITH A TWIST OF RAYON IN A MYSTERIOSO MIDNIGHT BLUE. FOR A SUBTLE, IRRESISTIBLE SPARKLE, DO THE OPTIONAL ALL-OVER BEADING AS YOU GO, SO THERE'S NO NEED TO STRING THE BEADS FIRST.

SKILL LEVEL: EXPERIENCED ✦ ✦ ✦ ✦

SIZE

XS (S, M/L, XL, 2XL); finished bust 32 (36, 40, 45, 50)" (81 [91, 101.5, 114, 127]cm) to fit body bust up to 34 (38, 42, 47, 52)" (86 [96.5, 106.5, 119, 132] cm) with negative ease; sample shown is size XS

MATERIALS

Filatura Di Crosa Brilla; 42% cotton, 58% rayon; 1.75 oz (50g)/120 yd (110m) (DK) (**3**)

—9 (10, 12, 14, 15) balls in #306 Midnight Blue

Size H-8 (5mm) crochet hook

Split-ring markers or scraps of yarn for markers

Size 13/14 (0.9mm) steel crochet hook, for optional beading

Beads, 5–6mm diameter, 248 (268, 320, 354, 416) plus extra just in case, optional

GAUGE

12 Fsc = 4" (10cm)

In Lace Stitch Pattern, 1 repeat = 2¼" (5.5cm); 4 rows = 2" (5cm)

STITCHES USED

Fsc (see page 134 for technique), sl st, ch, sc, hdc, dc, tr

STITCH DEFINITIONS

SH (SHELL) [dc, ch 1, dc, ch 1, dc] all in the same stitch or space.

INC-SH (INCREASE SHELL) [dc, ch 1, dc, ch 1, dc, ch 1, dc] all in the same stitch or space.

BOB (DC2TOG BOBBLE) dc2tog in the same stitch or space.

For skirt doily lace stitch definitions and diagrams for lace pattern rounds, see Felina Skirt (page 89).

Lace Stitch Pattern (for dress body)

This is crocheted in rounds, with RS always facing, and with optional beads applied in every other row so that they rest on the top of the sc in the lace pattern. This means that the beads must be slipped onto the loop before making a sc. You may simply omit the beading and make each sc as usual.

—To work in lace stitch pattern even, use these four rounds.

PATT R Ch 1, Slip Bead, sc in the beginning sp, [ch 3, skip the next sc, SH in the next ch-1 sp, ch 3, Slip Bead, skip the next bobble, sc in the next ch-1 sp] around, except omit the last (ch 3, slip bead and sc), instead end with ch 2, sc in the beginning sc.

PATT S Ch 1, sc in the beginning sp, [ch 1, skip the next sc, sc in the next ch-3 sp, ch 3, Bob in the next ch-1 sp of the shell, ch 1, Bob in the next ch-1 sp of the shell, ch 3, sc in the next ch-3 sp] around, except omit the last sc, instead end with sl st in the beginning sc.

PATT T Sl st in the first ch-1 sp, ch 6 (counts as a dc, ch 3), Slip Bead, skip the next bobble, sc in the next ch-1 sp, [ch 3, skip the next sc, SH in the next ch-1 sp, ch 3, Slip Bead, skip the next

bobble, sc in the next ch-1 sp] around, end with ch 3, (dc, ch 1, dc) in the same sp as at the beginning, sc in the 3rd ch of the beginning ch to complete the beginning shell.

PATT U Ch 2, dc in the beginning sp for beginning bobble, [ch 3, sc in the next ch-3 sp, ch 1, skip the next sc, sc in the next ch-3 sp, ch 3, Bob in the next ch-1 sp of the shell, ch 1, Bob in the next ch-1 sp of the shell] around, except omit the last (ch 1, Bob), instead end with sc in the 2nd ch of the beginning ch.

Beading

I like the look of all-over beads in my lace projects, but I find the task of prestringing beads onto the yarn an annoyance. This technique allows you to place beads where you want them when you get there.

The work is easier with smooth and firmly twisted yarns, but all types and weights of yarn can be successfully beaded. Choose beads large enough that they won't get lost in the crochet stitches, with big enough holes for this technique. There are many types

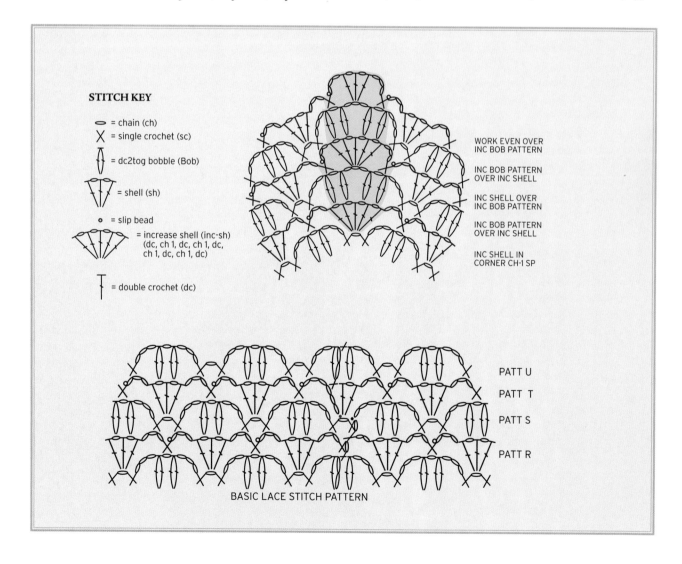

STITCH KEY

⬭ = chain (ch)

✕ = single crochet (sc)

⬍ = dc2tog bobble (Bob)

⟁ = shell (sh)

○ = slip bead

⬚ = increase shell (inc-sh)
(dc, ch 1, dc, ch 1, dc, ch 1, dc, ch 1, dc)

╪ = double crochet (dc)

WORK EVEN OVER INC BOB PATTERN

INC BOB PATTERN OVER INC SHELL

INC SHELL OVER INC BOB PATTERN

INC BOB PATTERN OVER INC SHELL

INC SHELL IN CORNER CH-1 SP

PATT U

PATT T

PATT S

PATT R

BASIC LACE STITCH PATTERN

of beads within the 5–6mm-diameter range that would be appropriate matches for this DK-weight yarn—E-type beads, pebble beads, small crow beads, round beads. The sample uses 5mm silver-lined glass cubes

SLIP BEAD On the work, drop the loop from the large hook. Slip one bead onto the steel hook. Insert the steel hook in the dropped loop, keeping a firm hold on the loop so that it doesn't enlarge. Apply some tension to the loop to keep it firmly against the tip of the steel hook. Using your right thumb, guide the bead down the hook and onto the loop and draw through only enough loop to accommodate the large hook. Reinsert the large hook, continue work, snugging up the next stitch to secure.

INSTRUCTIONS

This dress is crocheted with RS always facing. The lace stitch pattern begins with the joining of rounds slightly to the left of the first corner, but will shift to the center of the corner during the following rounds.

Yoke

Fsc 96 (96, 96, 99, 99), turn the foundation so the sc edge is on top, sl st in the beginning sc to form a ring, careful not to twist foundation, begin work across the sc edge.

Size XS

RND 1 Ch 4, [dc, ch 1, dc] for a shell in the first sc, [ch 3, Slip Bead, skip the next 2 sc, sc in the next sc, ch 3, skip the next 2 sc, SH in the next sc] 15 times, ch 3, Slip Bead, skip the next 2 sc, sc in the next sc, dc in the 3rd ch of the beginning ch—16 pattern repeats.

Sizes S and M/L

RND 1 Ch 4, [dc, ch 1, dc] for a shell in the first sc, ch 3, Slip Bead, skip the next sc, sc in the next sc, *[ch 3, skip the next 2 sc, SH in the next sc, ch 3, Slip Bead, skip the next 2 sc, sc in the next sc] twice, ch 3, skip the next sc, SH in the next sc, ch 3, Slip Bead, skip the next sc, sc in the next sc*; repeat from * to * 4 times, repeat between [ ] twice, end with dc in the 3rd ch of the beginning ch—18 pattern repeats.

Sizes XL and 2XL

RND 1 Ch 4, [dc, ch 1, dc] for a shell in the first sc, [ch 3, Slip Bead, skip the next 2 sc, sc in the next sc, ch 3, skip the next sc, SH in the next sc] 19 times, ch 3, Slip Bead, skip the next sc, sc in the next sc, skip the last sc, dc in the 3rd ch of the beginning ch—20 pattern repeats.

All Sizes

RND 2 Ch 1, sc in the beginning sp, [ch 3, Bob in the next ch-1 sp of the shell, ch 1, Bob in the next ch-1 sp of the shell, ch 3, sc in the next ch-3 sp, ch 1, sc in the next ch-3 sp] around, except omit the last (ch 1, sc), instead end with sc in the beginning sc.

RND 3 Ch 4, dc in the beginning sp, [ch 3, Slip Bead, sc in the next ch-1 sp, ch 3, SH in the next ch-1 sp] 4 (5, 5, 6, 6) times, *ch 3, Slip Bead, sc in the next ch-1 sp, ch 3, INC-SH in the next ch-1 sp for a corner*, repeat between [ ] twice, repeat from * to * once for a corner, repeat between [ ] 4 (5, 5, 6) times, repeat from * to * once for a corner, repeat between [ ] twice, ch 3, Slip Bead, sc in the next ch-1 sp, ch 3, end with SH in the same sp as at the beginning to complete the beginning corner, sc in the 3rd ch of the beginning ch. **Mark the middle stitch at each of four corners; move or wrap markers up as you go.**

RND 4 Ch 2, dc in the beginning sp, ch 1, Bob in the next ch-1 sp, ch 3, sc in the next ch-3 sp, ch 1, sc in the next ch-3 sp, ch 3, *[Bob in the next ch-1 sp of the shell, ch 1, Bob in the next ch-1 sp of the shell, ch 3, sc in the next ch-3 sp, ch 1, sc in the next ch-3 sp, ch 3] across to the next corner, over the increase shell work Bob in the first ch-1 sp, ch 1, Bob in the next ch-1 sp, ch 3, Bob in the next ch-1 sp, ch 1, Bob in the next ch-1 sp, ch 3, sc in the next ch-3 sp, ch 1, sc in the next ch-3 sp, ch 3*; repeat from * to * twice, repeat between [ ] across to the last corner, end with Bob in the first ch-1 sp of the increase shell, ch 1, Bob in the next ch-1 sp, ch 1, hdc in the 2nd ch of the beginning ch to complete the beginning corner.

Size XS and S

RND 5 Ch 6, Slip Bead, skip the next bobble, sc in the next ch-1 sp, *[ch 3, SH in the next ch-1 sp, ch 3, Slip Bead, sc in the next ch-1 sp] across to ch-3 sp at the middle of the next corner, ch 3, SH in the corner ch-3 sp, ch 3, Slip Bead, sc in the next ch-1 sp*; repeat from * to * twice, repeat between [ ] across to the beginning corner, ch 3, (dc, ch 1, dc) in the same corner ch-sp as at the beginning, sc in the 3rd ch of the beginning ch to complete the beginning shell—20 (22) pattern repeats.

RND 6 Work Patt U.

RND 7 Work Patt R.

RND 8 Work Patt S.

Sizes M/L and XL

RND 5 Ch 4, dc in the beginning ch-sp, ch 3, Slip Bead, skip the next bobble, sc in the next ch-1 sp, *[ch 3, SH in the next ch-1 sp, ch 3, Slip Bead, sc in the next ch-1 sp] across to ch-3 sp at the middle of the next corner, ch 3, INC-SH in corner ch-3 sp, ch 3,

Slip Bead, sc in the next ch-1 sp*; repeat from * to * twice, repeat between [ ] across to the beginning corner, ch 3, SH in the same corner ch-sp as at the beginning, sc in the 3rd ch of the beginning ch to complete the beginning corner.

RND 6 Repeat Rnd 4.

RNDS 7–10 Same as size XS Rnds 5–8—26 (28) pattern repeats.

Size 2XL

RND 5 Same as size M/L Rnd 5.

RND 6 Repeat Rnd 4.

RND 7 Repeat Rnd 5.

RND 8 Repeat Rnd 4.

RNDS 9–12 Same as size XS Rnds 5–8—32 pattern repeats.

Body

All sizes have (sc, ch 1, sc) at each of the four corners. Join the front and back at the underarms, making one continuous round by adding stitches at each underarm.

RND 1 (JOIN UNDERARMS) Sl st in the first ch-1 sp, ch 6, *work in stitch pattern as established to the next corner ch-1 sp, SH in corner ch-1 sp, ch 1, Fsc 7 for underarm, skip the next 3 (3, 4, 4, 5) repeats of (sc, ch-1, sc)*, SH in ch-1 sp of the next corner; repeat from * to * once, end with (dc, ch 1, dc) in the same sp as at the beginning, sc in the 3rd ch of the beginning ch.

RND 2 Ch 2, dc in the beginning ch-sp, *work in stitch pattern as established to the shell before the next underarm foundation, Bob in the first ch-1 sp of the shell, ch 1, Bob in the next ch-1 sp of the shell, ch 3, skip the next 2 sc of the underarm, sc in the next sc, ch 1, skip the next sc, sc in the next sc, ch 3, skip the remaining 2 sc of the underarm, Bob in the next ch-1 sp of the shell past the underarm*; repeat from * to * once, end with sc in the 2nd ch of the beginning ch—14 (16, 18, 20, 22) pattern repeats.

RNDS 3–22 Work [Patt R, Patt S, Patt T, Patt U] 5 times.

> *Fit Tip*
>
> Lengthen or shorten the dress body here before continuing with the skirt. Add or omit pattern rows as desired, end by working a Patt S or Patt U.

Skirt

For a full, swirly skirt, add rounds of doily lace, similar to Felina (page 88). There are 28 (32, 36, 40, 44) ch-1 sps in the last round of the body. Each repeat of the doily lace is worked across 4 of those ch-1 sps. To get the lace repeats nicely centered around the body, sizes XS, M/L, and 2XL continue with the last loop. Sizes S and XL fasten off after the last round of the body, skip the next ch-1 sp, join yarn with sl st in the next ch-1 sp. Continue with RS always facing.

RND 1 Ch 3, tr in the same ch-1 sp, [ch 3, V in the next ch-1 sp] 27 (31, 35, 39, 43) times, end with ch 3, Cl in the same ch-sp as at the beginning, ch 1, hdc in the 3rd ch of the beginning ch—28 (32, 36, 40, 44) Vs to make 7 (8, 9, 10, 11) lace repeats.

RNDS 2–12 Work in the same way as Felina Skirt (page 88) Rnds 5–15.

Sleeves

With RS facing, join yarn in the 4th ch at the center of one underarm foundation and make a tiny sleeve around the armhole. Omit bead in the sc at the center of the underarm.

RND 1 Ch 1, sc in the same ch, ch 3, skip 3 ch of the foundation, SH in the next dc row edge past the underarm, work in stitch pattern with beads as established, making 4 (4, 5, 5, 6) shells, placing the last SH in the next dc row edge before the underarm foundation, ch 2, sc in the beginning sc—5 (5, 6, 6, 7) pattern repeats.

RNDS 2–6 Work as [Patt S, Patt T, Patt U, Patt R, Patt S].

> *Fit Tip*
>
> Lengthen or shorten sleeves here before edging by adding or omitting pattern rounds as desired; end by working a Patt S or Patt U.

EDGING Make a scallop of (sl st, ch 2, hdc) in the first ch-1 sp, [scallop in the next ch-3 sp, scallop in the next ch-1 sp] around, end with sl st in the same ch-1 sp as at the beginning, fasten off. Make sleeve and edging around the other armhole in the same way. Lengthen or shorten sleeves here before edging by adding or omitting pattern rounds as desired; end by working a Patt S or Patt U.

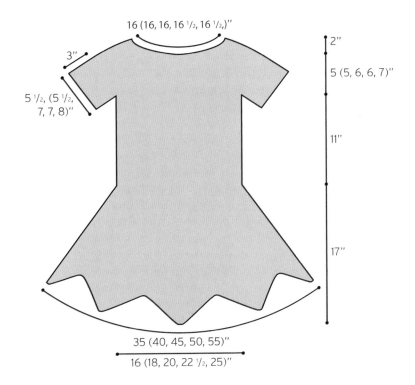

16 (16, 16, 16 1/2, 16 1/2)"

3"

2"

5 (5, 6, 6, 7)"

5 1/2, (5 1/2, 7, 7, 8)"

11"

17"

35 (40, 45, 50, 55)"

16 (18, 20, 22 1/2, 25)"

Neckline

Finish the neckline with a round of scallop edging.

Join yarn with sl st in the beginning ch of the neck foundation.

EDGING Ch 2, hdc in the same ch, skip the next 2 ch, [make a scallop of (sl st, ch 2, hdc) in the next ch, skip the next 2 ch] around, end with sl st in the same ch as at the beginning, fasten off. Weave in ends, block dress.

Fit Tip

The neckline may stretch out with blocking. If it gets too loose for your taste, here's a retro-fix. After blocking, with wrong-side facing, make a round of slip stitch, one sl st in each ch of the neck foundation, working as firmly as needed to hold in some of the fullness, and switching to a smaller hook if necessary.

ISABEAU TOP &
ISABEAU TUNISIAN BELT

· ——— ·· ✦ ·· ——— ·

IF THE BOZENA DRESS IS A STUNNER BY NIGHT, THEN ISABEAU SOARS BY DAY. BY LEAVING OFF THE SKIRT, THE SAME DRESS BODICE ELONGATES INTO A SLEEK, PRETTY LACE TOP, EDGED WITH BEADED TRIM AS SHOWN IN THE SAMPLE HERE, OR WITH THE ALL-OVER BEADED OPTION AS DESCRIBED FOR THE DRESS. WITH LONGER SLEEVES AND BODY, ISABEAU IS MORE FORGIVING AND EASIER FOR MOST BODIES TO WEAR. THE LENGTH IS PERFECT FOR WRAPPING WITH THE MATCHING TUNISIAN BELT TO ACCENTUATE YOUR WAIST.

SKILL LEVEL: EXPERIENCED ✦ ✦ ✦ ✦

TOP

SIZE
XS (S, M/L, XL, 2XL); finished bust 32 (36, 40, 45, 50)" (81 [91, 101.5, 114, 127]cm) to fit body bust up to 34 (38, 42, 47, 52)" (86 [96.5, 106.5, 119, 132] cm) with negative ease; sample shown is size XS

MATERIALS
NaturallyCaron.com Spa; 75% micro-denier acrylic, 25% bamboo; 3 oz (85g)/ 251 yd (230m) (Sport/DK) (3)

—4 (5, 6, 6, 7) skeins (makes both top and following belt) in #0007 Naturally

Size I-9 (5.5mm) crochet hook

Split-ring markers or scraps of yarn for markers

Size 13/14 (0.9mm) steel crochet hook, for optional beading

Beads, 5–6mm diameter, 120 (126, 138, 146, 158) beads, plus extra just in case, optional

GAUGE
12 Fsc = 4" (10cm)

In Lace Stitch Pattern, 1 repeat = 2¼" (5.5cm); 4 rows = 2" (5cm)

STITCHES USED
Fsc (see page 134 for technique), sl st, ch, sc, hdc, dc, dc3tog, tr

For stitch definitions, lace stitch pattern rows for body, and notes about beading, see Bozena Dress (page 96).

BELT
SIZE
1¾" (4.5cm) wide; 54" (137cm) long or length desired.

MATERIALS
Same yarn as Isabeau Top, approximately 1 oz (28g) (more yarn needed for longer belt)

Size H-8 (5mm) crochet hook

Size I-9 (5.5mm) Tunisian crochet hook or makeshift tool

Size 13/14 (0.9mm) steel crochet hook, for beading

6 beads, same as used in Isabeau Top

GAUGE
This is a much firmer gauge than used in the Isabeau Top, for a belt with some body.

16 sc = 4" (10cm)

In Tunisian Shell Pattern, 2 shells = 1" (2.5cm); 4 rows (F and R) = 2" (5cm)

STITCHES USED
Fsc (see page 134 for technique), sl st, ch, sc, dc3tog, tr

For notes about beading technique, see Isabeau Top (page 104).

For stitch definitions, Tunisian Shell Pattern rows, and stitch diagrams, and

for basic information about how to make Tunisian fabric, see the Tunisian Tutorial (page 54).

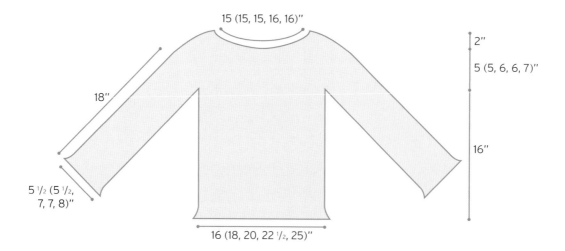

15 (15, 15, 16, 16)"

18"

2"

5 (5, 6, 6, 7)"

16"

5 ¹/₂ (5 ¹/₂, 7, 7, 8)"

16 (18, 20, 22 ¹/₂, 25)"

INSTRUCTIONS (FOR TOP)
Yoke

Refer to the top half of the Bozena Dress (page 96), make the yoke in the same way, omitting beading, except sizes XL and 2XL will have one small adjustment in the neckline. Call me obsessive, but I like to see the neckline trim come out even!

Sizes XS (S, M/L)

RNDS 1–8 (8, 10) Make in the same way as Bozena Dress Yoke (page 99) Rnds 1–8 (8, 10).

Sizes XL and 2XL

Fsc 100 instead of 99.

RND 1 Make in the same way as Bozena Dress Yoke (page 99) Rnd 1, except skip the last 2 sc before the end of the round.

RNDS 2–10 (12) Make in the same way as Bozena Dress Yoke (page 99) Rnds 2–10 (12).

Body (All Sizes)

RNDS 1–22 Make in the same way as Bozena Dress Body (page 97) Rnds 1–22, end by working a Patt U.

RNDS 23–32 Work 10 more rounds even, as [Patt R, Patt S, Patt T, Patt U] for 2 times, then [Patt R, Patt S] once more, fasten off.

> *Fit Tip*
>
> Lengthen or shorten the top here before continuing with the beaded trim by adding or omitting pattern rounds as desired; end by working a Patt S. You may also end with a Patt U, but instead of fastening off, continue with trim.

Beaded Trim

RND 1 With RS still facing, join with sl st in the next ch-1 sp between bobbles, ch 1, sc in the same sp, *ch 2, [tr, ch 2] 4 times in the next ch-1 sp, sc in the next ch-1 sp*; repeat from * to * 13 (15, 17, 19, 21) times around, except omit the last sc, end with sl st in the beginning sc.

RND 2 Ch 1, sc in the same sc, *[ch 3, Slip Bead, skip the next tr, dc3tog in the next ch-2 sp] 3 times, ch 3, sc in the next sc*; repeat from * to * around, except omit the last sc, end with sl st in the beginning sc, fasten off.

Sleeves (All Sizes)

RNDS 1–6 Make in the same way as Bozena Dress Sleeves (page 100) Rnds 1–6, ending with a Patt S.

RNDS 7–36 Work 30 more rounds even, as [Patt T, Patt U, Patt R, Patt S] for 7 times, then work [Patt T, Patt U] once more.

> *Fit Tip*
>
> Lengthen or shorten the sleeve before making the beaded trim by adding or omitting pattern rounds as desired; end by working a Patt U. You may also end with a Patt S, then fasten off, join in the next ch-1 sp and continue with trim.

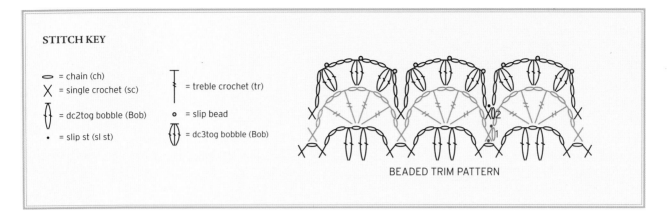

STITCH KEY

◯ = chain (ch)
✗ = single crochet (sc)
⬥ = dc2tog bobble (Bob)
• = slip st (sl st)

⊺ = treble crochet (tr)
∘ = slip bead
⬥ = dc3tog bobble (Bob)

BEADED TRIM PATTERN

Beaded Trim

RND 1 Ch 1, sc in the same sp, *ch 2, [tr, ch 2] 4 times in the next ch-1 sp, sc in the next ch-1 sp*; repeat from * to * 4 (4, 5, 5, 6) times around, except omit the last sc, end with sl st in the beginning sc.

RND 2 Make in the same way as Body Beaded Trim Rnd 2.

Make sleeve and beaded trim around the other armhole in the same way.

Beaded Neckline

This trim allows you to adjust the neck opening if it is too loose, as the slip stitches tend to be firm. If you prefer a looser neckline, keep the stitches in the trim round as relaxed as possible.

BEADED TRIM With RS facing, join yarn with sl st in the first ch of the neck foundation, [ch 1, Slip Bead, ch 1, skip the next ch, sl st in the next ch] around, ending with sl st in the same ch as at the beginning, fasten off.

Weave in ends, block top.

INSTRUCTIONS (FOR BELT)

Using the regular crochet hook, Fsc 8 firmly, put the last loop on the Tunisian hook, turn the foundation so the sc edge is on top.

ROW 1-F(ORWARD) Same as Tunisian Tutorial First Forward Pass (page 54) for 7 more loops, inserting hook through the back loop only of each foundation sc—8 loops.

ROW 1-R(ETURN) Same as Tunisian Tutorial First Return Row, (page 54) Normal Tunisian Return.

ROW 2-F Ch 2, skip the first vertical bar of edge stitch, skip the next st, Tsh in the next st inserting hook as if to Tks, skip the next 2 st, Tsh in the next st inserting hook as if to Tks, skip the next st, Ttd into edge stitch—8 loops.

ROW 2-R Normal return.

ROW 3-F Work Tss—8 loops.

ROW 3-R Normal return.

Repeat (Row 2-F, Row 2-R, Row 3-F, Row 3-R) 49 times or for desired length.

Finishing

Put the last loop onto the regular crochet hook, make the sc edging and beaded trim in one.

FIRST END Ch 1, inserting hook as if to Tks, sc in each of 8 st across, turn. Ch 1, sc in the first sc, ch 2, skip the next 2 sc, [tr, ch 2] 4 times in the next sc, skip the next 3 sc, sc in the last sc, turn. *[Ch 3, Slip Bead, dc3tog in the next ch-2 sp] 3 times, ch 3, sc in row edge of the last sc, sc in the next sc row edge. Along Tunisian row edges work [sc in each Tss row edge, 3 sc in each Ttd row edge] across the long side of the belt, end with sc in the beginning Tss row edge at the other end of the belt*, sc in the Fsc row edge, rotate, sc in the first ch of the foundation, ch 2, skip the next 2 ch, [tr, ch 2] 4 times in the next ch, skip the next 3 ch, sc in the last ch, turn. Repeat from * to * once, end with sc in the next sc row edge, sl st in the next sc row edge, fasten off.

Weave in ends.

Exploded Lace Trim

Happy Endings

LOVELY LITTLE EDGINGS WERE AND CONTINUE TO BE AN important part of a thread crocheter's arsenal. When exploded to use thicker yarns and bigger hooks, many thread edgings originally added to hankies, towels, and bed linens become bold statements as garment trims.

The lace for the designs in this chapter was adapted from a lace collar I saw in a vintage Japanese crochet book. Of the few books that my mother brought with her to this country fifty years ago, it is the only one that survives. Written in Japanese, the text of this yellowing volume is indecipherable by me; however, thanks to the photos and international symbol diagrams, I can continue to re-create and enjoy the crochet. Look through your own collection of vintage and new lace books and you'll start to see those edgings and trims in a fresh, exploded way. Then let the designs in this chapter inspire you to lace up your own creations.

LING COLLAR

IT SOUNDS IDIOTIC THAT I SHOULD TAKE THE ORIGINAL TINY, HIGH-NECK THREAD COLLAR, DISSECT AND EXPLODE THE STITCHES, THEN TURN AROUND AND REVERSE-ENGINEER IT BACK INTO A COLLAR. SO I AM AN IDIOT, BUT A HAPPY ONE. THE BRILLIANT SILVER OF THIS OVERSIZED COLLAR (OR UNDERSIZED PONCHO, DEPENDING ON YOUR PERSPECTIVE) WOULD BE EQUALLY STUNNING OVER A PLAIN TOP OR OVER BARE SHOULDERS. THE OPTIONAL BEADS ON EACH LACE POINT, RATHER LIKE JEWELS, GIVE THIS NEARLY WEIGHTLESS METALLIC YARN SOME EXTRA SWING. LING IS MUCH LESS FUSSY AND FRILLY THAN THE ORIGINAL, BUT NO LESS ALLURING.

SKILL LEVEL: EASY ✦ ✦ ✦ ✦

SIZE
Finished neck 28" (71cm); finished lower edge 56" (142cm); length 9" (23cm)

MATERIALS
Filatura Di Crosa New Smoking; 65% viscose, 35% polyester; 0.88 oz (25g)/132 yd (120m)

(fine) 〔1〕

—2 balls in #02 Silver

Size H-8 (5mm) crochet hook

Size 13/14 (0.9mm) steel crochet hook, for optional beading

8 beads, with holes large enough for technique

I used foil-lined 7mm round glass beads. Since you need only eight, and they will act as weights, you can use semiprecious stones or jewelry-grade beads if you like, larger and heavier than suggested for previous beaded projects.

GAUGE
14 Fsc = 4" (10cm)

For stitches used, stitch definitions and lace stitch diagram, see Ming Jacket (page 110).

For working lace border in rounds, see Ping Skirt (page 116).

For notes about beading, see Bozena Dress (page 96).

INSTRUCTIONS

Fsc 96, turn foundation so the sc edge is on top, sl st in the beginning sc to form a ring, careful not to twist stitches; begin work across the sc edge.

RND 1 (RS) Ch 6 (counts as a dc, ch 3), skip the same sc, skip the next sc, [dc in the next sc, ch 3, skip the next sc] around, end with sl st in the 3rd ch of the beginning ch—48 ch-3 sp.

RND 2 (RS) Ch 3, 2 dc in the first ch-3 sp, 3 dc in each of the next 47 ch-3 sp, end with sl st in the 3rd ch of the beginning ch, turn—144 dc.

Using the same pattern as Ping Skirt (page 116) for lace border in rounds, make 8 lace pattern repeats around.

RNDS 3–13 Make in the same way as Ping Skirt (page 116) Border Trim, Rnds 3–13.

For the optional beaded trim, omit Rnd 13, instead work the following round that replaces each Picot with a slipped bead.

BEADED RND 13 (RS) Ch 1, Slip Bead, 3 sc in the beginning sp, *3 sc in each of the next 11 ch-3 sp, [2 sc, Slip Bead, 3 sc] in ch-3 sp of the next V*; repeat from * to * around, except end with 2 sc in the same ch-sp as at the beginning, sl st in the beginning sc, fasten off.

Finishing (optional)

NECK EDGING (RS) With RS of collar facing, join yarn with sl st in the first foundation chain, ch 1, moving from left to right backwards, [rev sc in the next ch, ch 1, skip next ch] around, end with sl st in the beginning sc, fasten off.
Weave in ends, block collar.

Fit Tip

If the neckline has stretched too much and is too loose, crochet the neck edging more firmly to gather in as much of the fullness as desired, switching to a smaller hook if needed. Or weave a length of narrow ribbon or drawstring through the chain-3 spaces at the neck, gather and tie.

MING JACKET

◆ ── •• ✦ •• ── •

IF I HAD TO CHOOSE THE PIECES FROM THIS BOOK THAT BEST EXEMPLIFY WHAT I DO WITH CROCHET, THIS MING JACKET AND THE MATCHING PING SKIRT WOULD BE THE ONES. FROM THE MOMENT I FIRST PUT MY HOOK TO THIS LUXURY HEMP YARN, I KNEW THAT IT WAS DESTINED TO BECOME A GORGEOUS SUIT. WORKED FROM THE GARMENT 101 TEMPLATES (PAGE 118), THE MING JACKET STOPS AT EMPIRE LENGTH; THE PING SKIRT REACHES TO MIDTHIGH. FROM THERE BOTH PIECES FLOW INTO THE SAME LACE AS THE LING COLLAR, ONLY HERE THE ORIGINAL THREE INCHES (7.5CM) OF THREAD LACE GET MAXIMUM EXPLOSION INTO A THIRTEEN-INCH (33cm) DEEP LACE BORDER.

MING IS A MINIMALLY SHAPED JACKET, BUT THAT DOES NOT MEAN IT IS SHAPELESS. THE LOW, GRACEFUL V-NECK AND OPEN FRONT DRAW THE EYE TO THE LACE, WHICH DRAPES THE WAIST AND FLARES TO PRETTY POINTS ALL AROUND. WITH TOP-OF-THE-HIP LENGTH AND FITTED THREE-QUARTER-LENGTH SLEEVES, MING HAS THE PERFECT PROPORTIONS TO WEAR WITH THE SLIM, BELOW-THE-KNEE PING SKIRT THAT FOLLOWS.

SKILL LEVEL: EXPERIENCED ◆ ◆ ◆ ◆

SIZE

XS (S, M, L, XL, 2XL, 3XL); finished bust 33 (36, 39, 42, 45, 48, 51)" (84 [91, 99, 106.5, 114, 122, 129.5]cm) to fit body bust up to 34 (37, 40, 43, 46, 49, 52)" (86 [94, 101.5, 109, 117, 124.5, 132] cm) with a bit of negative ease; sample shown is size XS

MATERIALS

Lanaknits HempForKnitting Allhemp-6LUX (#102-L); 100% Hemp; 3.5 oz (100g)/143 yd (130m) (DK weight) 🧵

—5 (5, 6, 6, 7, 7, 8) hanks in #057 Ice

Size I-9 (5.5mm) crochet hook

Split-ring markers or contrasting yarn for markers

GAUGE (AS CROCHETED)

11 Fsc or sc = 4" (10cm)

In shell stitch pattern, 2 repeats of (shell, sc) = 3" (7.5cm), 4 rows = 2¼" (5.5cm) (will lengthen with blocking to 4 rows = 2½" [6.5cm] or more)

In Mesh Trim at underbust or sleeve trim, 4 repeats of (dc, ch 2) = 2¾" (7cm)

STITCHES USED

Fsc (see page 134), sl st, ch, sc, dc, dc2tog, dc3tog

STITCH DEFINITIONS

SH (SHELL) (dc, ch 1, dc, ch 1, dc) all in the same stitch or space.

INC-SH (INCREASE SHELL) (dc, ch 1, dc, ch 1, dc, ch 1, dc) all in the same stitch or space.

V (dc, ch 3, dc) all in the same stitch or space.

V IN V (dc, ch 3, dc) in ch-3 sp of the next V.

PICOT After completing a sc, ch 3, reach back and insert hook from top to bottom through the front loop of the sc just made AND through one forward strand of the stem (in other words, retrace the path of the loop that closed the sc), YO and sl st to close Picot.

For Basic Shell Stitch Patterns and the ways to increase and decrease, in rows and in rounds, see the explanations in Jacket 101 (page 120).

INSTRUCTIONS
Yoke

ROWS 1–11 (12, 12, 13, 13, 14, 14) Make in the same way as Jacket 101 (page 120) Yoke Rows 1–11 (12, 12, 13, 13, 14, 14).

Body

ROWS 1–5 Join at the underarms, insert the wedge for bust shaping if desired, complete the V-neck shaping, then continue to work even (without increasing or decreasing) in the same way as the Jacket 101 Body Rows 1–5, ending by working as Patt A (B, A, B, A, B, B)—22 shells (23 shells plus half-shells at ends, 26 shells, 27 shells plus half-shells at ends, 30 shells, 31 shells plus half-shells at ends, 33 shells plus half-shells at ends).

Fit Tip

To shorten the empire waist body before the lace border, omit rows as desired. To lengthen the empire waist body before the lace border, add a row or rows in pattern, alternating Patt A and/or Patt B as needed.

Lace Border

This border requires 18 stitches for each lace repeat, plus one edge stitch. In order to fit the needed number of repeats around the jacket and still create a slight taper at the underbust, a certain amount of calculating has been done to adjust the stitch count. All sizes turn, WS now facing.

Sizes XS (M, XL)

ROW 1 (WS) Ch 5 (counts as dc, ch 2), [dc in the 2nd dc of the next shell, ch 2, dc in the next sc, ch 2] across, except omit the last ch 2, end by placing the last dc in the last sc, turn—44 (52, 60) ch-2 sp.

Sizes S (L, 2XL, 3XL)

ROW 1 (WS) Ch 5, [dc in the next sc, ch 2, dc in the 2nd dc of the next shell, ch 2] across, except omit the last ch 2, end by placing the last dc in the 3rd ch of tch, turn—48 (56, 64, 68) ch-2 sp.
Mark the dc at dead center of the back to make it easier to the center the lace repeats.

Size XS

ROW 2 (RS) Ch 3, 2 dc in each of the next 22 ch-2 sp to the center back, dc in the center back dc, 2 dc in each of the next 22 ch-2 sp to the end, dc in the 3rd ch of tch, turn—91 dc.

Size S

ROW 2 (RS) Ch 3, [2 dc in each of the next 5 ch-2 sp, dc in the next ch-2 sp] 4 times to the center back, dc in the center back dc, [dc in the next ch-2 sp, 2 dc in each of the next 5 ch-2 sp] 4 times to the end, dc in the 3rd ch of tch, turn—91 dc.

Size M

ROW 2 (RS) Ch 3, 2 dc in each of the next 25 ch-2 sp, 3 dc in the next ch-2 sp, dc in the center back dc, 3 dc in the next ch-2 sp, 2 dc in each of the next 25 ch-2 sp to the end, dc in the 3rd ch of tch, turn—109 dc.

Size L

ROW 2 (RS) Ch 3, 2 dc in the first ch-2 sp, [dc in the next ch-2 sp, 2 dc in each of the next 8 ch-2 sp] 3 times to the center back, dc in the center back dc, [2 dc in each of the next 8 ch-2 sp, dc in the next ch-2 sp] 3 times, 2 dc in the last sp, dc in the 3rd ch of tch, turn—109 dc.

Size XL

ROW 2 (RS) Ch 3, [2 dc in each of the next 14 ch-2 sp, 3 dc in the next ch-2 sp] 2 times to the center back, dc in the center back dc, [3 dc in the next ch-2 sp, 2 dc in each of the next 14 ch-2 sp] 2 times to the end, dc in the 3rd ch of tch, turn—127 dc.

Size 2XL

ROW 2 (RS) Ch 3, [2 dc in each of the next 15 ch-2 sp, dc in the next ch-2 sp] 2 times to the center back, dc in the center back dc, [dc in the next ch-2 sp, 2 dc in each of the next 15 ch-2 sp] 2 times to the end, dc in the 3rd ch of tch, turn—127 dc.

Size 3XL

ROW 2 (RS) Ch 3, 2 dc in the first ch-2 sp, [2 dc in each of the next 10 ch-2 sp, 3 dc in the next ch-2 sp] 3 times to the center back, dc in the center back dc, [3 dc in the next ch-2 sp, 2 dc in each of the next 10 ch-2 sp] 3 times, 2 dc in the last sp, dc in the 3rd ch of tch, turn—145 dc.

All Sizes

Make 5 (5, 6, 6, 7, 7, 8) lace repeats over 91 (91, 109, 109, 127, 127, 145) stitches.

ROW 3 (WS) Ch 3, skip the first dc, dc in the next dc, *ch 6, skip the next 2 dc, sc in each of the next 11 dc, ch 6, skip the next 2 dc, dc in each of the next 3 dc*; repeat from * to * 4 (4, 5, 5, 6, 6, 7) times, except omit the last dc, end with dc in the top of tch, turn.

ROW 4 Ch 3, skip the first dc, dc in the next dc, *dc in the next ch-6 sp, ch 6, skip the next sc, sc in each of the next 9 sc, ch 6, dc in the next

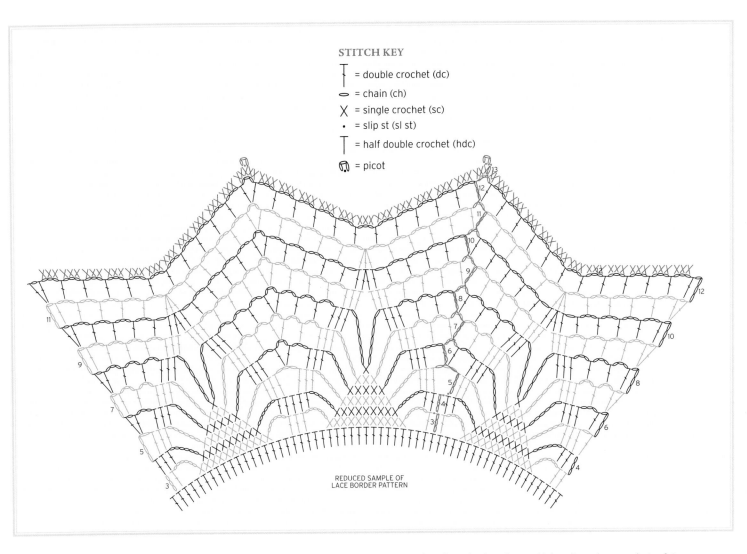

STITCH KEY

┬ = double crochet (dc)

⌒ = chain (ch)

✕ = single crochet (sc)

· = slip st (sl st)

┬ = half double crochet (hdc)

🪢 = picot

REDUCED SAMPLE OF
LACE BORDER PATTERN

ch-6 sp, dc in each of the next 3 dc*; repeat from * to * across, except omit the last dc, end with dc in the top of tch, turn.

ROW 5 Ch 4 (counts as dc, ch 1), skip the first dc, *dc in each of the next 2 dc, dc in the next ch-6 sp, ch 6, skip the next sc, sc in each of the next 7 sc, ch 6, dc in the next ch-6 sp, dc in each of the next 2 dc, ch 3, skip the next dc*; repeat from * to * across, except omit the last ch 3, instead end with ch 1, dc in the 3rd ch of tch, turn.

ROW 6 Ch 4, dc in the first ch-1 sp, *ch 3, skip the next dc, dc in each of the next 2 dc, dc in the next ch-6 sp, ch 6, skip the next sc, sc in each of the next 5 sc, ch 6, dc in the next ch-6 sp, dc in each of the next 2 dc, ch 3, V in the next ch-3 sp*; repeat from * to * across, except omit the last V, instead end with (dc, ch 1, dc) in tch sp, turn.

ROW 7 Ch 4, dc in the first ch-1 sp, *ch 3, dc in the next ch-3 sp, ch 3, skip the next dc, dc in each of the next 2 dc, dc in the next ch-6 sp, ch 6, skip the next sc, sc in each of the next 3 sc, ch 6, dc in the next ch-6 sp, dc in each of the next 2 dc, ch 3, dc in the next ch-3 sp, ch 3, V in the next V*; repeat from * to * across, except omit the last V, instead end with (dc, ch 1, dc) in tch sp, turn.

ROW 8 Ch 4, dc in the first ch-1 sp, *[ch 3, dc in the next ch-3 sp] 2 times, ch 3, skip the next dc, dc in each of the next 2 dc, dc in the next ch-6 sp, ch 6, skip the next sc, sc in the next sc, ch 6, dc in the next ch-6 sp, dc in each of the next 2 dc, [ch 3, dc in the next ch-3 sp] 2 times, ch 3, V in V*; repeat from * to * across, except omit the last V, instead end with (dc, ch 1, dc) in tch sp, turn.

ROW 9 Ch 4, dc in the first ch-1 sp, *[ch 3, dc in the next ch-3 sp] 3 times, ch 3, skip the next dc, dc in each of the next 2 dc, dc in the next ch-6 sp, skip the next sc, dc in the next ch-6 sp, dc in each of the next 2 dc, [ch 3, dc in the next ch-3 sp] 3 times, ch 3, V in V*; repeat from * to * across, except omit the last V, instead end with (dc, ch 1, dc) in tch sp, turn.

ROW 10 Ch 4, dc in the first ch-1 sp, *[ch 3, dc in the next ch-3 sp] 4 times, ch 1, skip the next dc, dc in the next dc, dc2tog in the next 2 dc, dc in the next dc, ch 1, [dc in the next ch-3 sp, ch 3] 4 times, V in V*; repeat from * to * across, except omit the last V, instead end with (dc, ch 1, dc) in tch sp, turn.

ROW 11 Ch 4, dc in the first ch-1 sp, *[ch 3, dc in the next ch-3 sp] 4 times, ch 3, skip the next ch-1 sp, dc3tog in the next 3 dc, ch 3, skip the next ch-1 sp, [dc in the next ch-3 sp, ch 3] 4 times, V in V*; repeat from * to * across, except omit the last V, instead end with (dc, ch 1, dc) in tch sp, turn.

ROW 12 (RS) Ch 4, dc in the first ch-1 sp, *[ch 3, dc in the next ch-3 sp] 10 times, ch 3, V in V*; repeat from * to * across, except omit the last V, instead end with (dc, ch 1, dc) in tch sp, do not turn.

Body Edging

With RS still facing, rotate and begin to sc evenly around the entire front and neck edges.

FRONT EDGE (RS) Ch 1, 3 sc in each of the next 12 row edges of the lace border, working evenly across row edges of shell stitch according to the progression for your size, make sc in each sc row edge, 2 sc in each dc row edge to the neck foundation; sc in each ch of the foundation, sc across the other front row edges in the same way, 3 sc in each of the 12 row edges of the lace border, rotate and finish the lower edge.

LOWER EDGE (RS) Sc in the 3rd ch of tch, Picot, 2 sc in the first ch-1 sp, *3 sc in each of the next 11 ch-3 sp, [3 sc, Picot, 2 sc] in ch-3 sp of the next V*; repeat from * to * across, except omit the last 2 sc, end with (3 sc, Picot) in the last ch-1 sp, sl st in the beginning sc, fasten off.

Sleeves

RNDS 1–16 Make a ¾-length tapered sleeve in the same way as Jacket 101 (page 120) Sleeve Rnds 1–16.

Fit Tip

To lengthen the sleeve before making the trim, add rounds in pattern, alternating [Patt N, Patt M] as desired.

Mesh Trim

RND 1 Ch 5, [dc in the 2nd dc of the next shell, ch 2, dc in the next sc] 6 (7, 7, 8, 8, 8, 9) times, except omit the last ch 2 and dc, instead end with ch 1, sc in the 3rd ch of the beginning ch, turn—12 (14, 14, 16, 16, 16, 18) ch-2 sp.

RND 2 Ch 5, [dc in the next ch-2 sp, ch 2] around, except omit the last ch-2, instead end with ch 1, sc in the 3rd ch of the beginning ch, turn.

RND 3 Repeat Rnd 2.

Work the last round of the sleeve edging with RS facing. Turn or do not turn based on the body edging for your size.

RND 20 (RS) Ch 1, sc in the first sp, 2 sc in each ch-2 sp around, end with sc in the same sp as at the beginning, sl st in the beginning sc, fasten off—24 (28, 28, 32, 32, 32, 36) sc.

Make sleeve around the other armhole in the same way.

Weave in ends, block jacket.

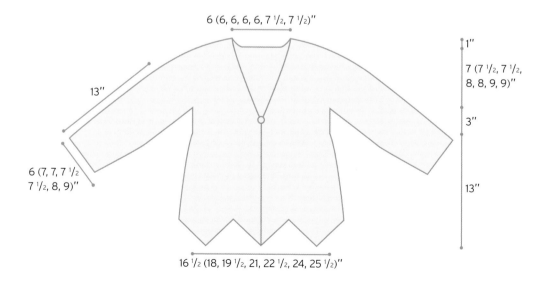

6 (6, 6, 6, 6, 7 ½, 7 ½)"

1"

7 (7 ½, 7 ½, 8, 8, 9, 9)"

13"

3"

6 (7, 7, 7 ½ 7 ½, 8, 9)"

13"

16 ½ (18, 19 ½, 21, 22 ½, 24, 25 ½)"

PING SKIRT

SIZE

XS (S, M, L, XL, 2XL); finished hip 8" (20.5cm) below waist 36 (39, 42, 45, 48, 51)" (91 [99, 106.5, 114, 122, 129.5]cm) to fit body hip up to 35 (38, 41, 44, 47, 50)" (90 [96.5, 104, 112, 119, 127]cm); sample shown is size XS

MATERIALS

Lanaknits Hemp For Knitting Allhemp6LUX (#102-L); 100% Hemp; 3.5 oz (100g)/143 yd (130m) (DK weight) ④

—5 (5, 6, 6, 7, 7) hanks in #057 Ice

Size I-9 (5.5mm) crochet hook

For no-sew elastic waist, 3 (3, 3, 4, 4, 4) yd/m ⅛" (3mm) narrow braided elastic

GAUGE (AS CROCHETED)

11 Fsc or sc = 4" (10cm)

In shell pattern of the skirt body: 2 repeats (shell, sc) = 3" (7.5cm); 4 rows = 2¼" (5.5cm)

For Basic Shell Stitch Pattern (in rounds), see Skirt 101 (page 129).

For stitches used, stitch definitions, lace border stitch rows, and diagram, see Ming Jacket (page 110).

INSTRUCTIONS

Skirt Yoke

RNDS 1–8 (8, 8, 9, 9, 9) Make in the same way as the Skirt 101 (page 129) Yoke Rnds 1–8 (8, 8, 9, 9, 9).

Skirt Body

RNDS 9 (9, 9, 10, 10, 10)–21 (21, 21, 23, 23, 23) Work even in shell stitch pattern for 13 (13, 13, 14, 14, 14) more rounds, or to the desired length before lace border, end by working a Patt M—24 (26, 28, 30, 32, 34) shells.

Lace Border

This is essentially the same lace border as the one on the Ming Jacket (page 110), except instead of working flat rows back and forth the skirt border is made in joined rounds back and forth. It requires 18 stitches for each lace repeat. In order to fit the needed number of repeats around the skirt and create a slight flare, a certain amount of calculating has been done to adjust the stitch count.

Turn, WS now facing.

All Sizes

RND 1 (WS) Ch 6 (counts as dc, ch 3), [dc in the 2nd dc of the next shell, ch 3, dc in the next sc, ch 3] around, except omit the last ch 3, instead end with ch 1, hdc in the 3rd ch of the beginning ch, turn—48 (52, 56, 60, 64, 68) ch-3 sps.

Sizes XS (L)

RND 2 (RS) Ch 3, dc in the beginning ch-sp, 3 dc in each of the next 47 (59) ch-3 sp, dc in the same sp as at the beginning, sl st in top of the beginning ch, turn—144 (180) dc.

Sizes S (XL)

RND 2 (RS) Ch 3, dc in the beginning ch-sp, [3 dc in each of the next 8 (10) ch-3 sp, 4 dc in the next ch-3 sp, 3 dc in each of the next 7 (9) ch-3 sp, 4 dc in the next ch-3 sp] 3 times, dc in the same sp as at the beginning, sl st in top of the beginning ch, turn—162 (198) dc.

Sizes M (2XL)

RND 2 (RS) Ch 3, dc in the beginning ch-sp, [3 dc in each of the next 8 (10) ch-3 sp, 2 dc in the next ch-3 sp] 6 times, 3 dc in the last ch-3 sp, dc in the same sp as at the beginning, sl st in top of the beginning ch, turn—162 (198) dc.

All Sizes

Make 8 (9, 9, 10, 11, 11) lace repeats over 144 (162, 162, 180, 198, 198) stitches. Rnds 3–12 correspond to Ming Jacket Lace (page 110). Border Rows 3–12 Convert the beginning and ending of each row into a joined round; make repeats from * to * for each corresponding round as needed.

RND 3 (WS) Ch 3 (counts as dc), skip the first dc, dc in the next dc, repeat Ming Lace Border Row 3 from * to * 8 (9, 9, 10, 11, 11) times, except omit the last 2 dc, end with sl st in the 3rd ch of the beginning ch, turn.

RND 4 Ch 3, skip the first dc, dc in the next dc, repeat Ming Lace Border Row 4 from * to * across, except omit the last 2 dc, end with sl st in the 3rd ch of the beginning ch, turn.

RND 5 Sl st in the next dc, ch 3, omit the first dc in the following repeat for the first time; repeat Ming Lace Border Row 5 from * to * around, except omit the last ch 3, instead end with ch 1, hdc in the 3rd ch of the beginning ch, turn.

RND 6–11 Ch 3, repeat Ming Lace Border Rows 6–11 from * to * around, except omit the last V, instead end with dc in the same sp as at the beginning, ch 1, hdc in the 3rd ch of the beginning ch, turn.

RND 12 (RS) Ch 3, repeat Ming Lace Border Row 12 from * to * around, except omit the last V, instead end with dc in the same sp as at the beginning, ch 1, hdc in the 3rd ch of the beginning ch, do not turn.

RND 13 (RS EDGING) Ch 1, sc, Picot, 2 sc in the beginning sp, *3 sc in each of the next 11 ch-3 sp, [3 sc, Picot, 2 sc] in ch-3 sp of the next V*; repeat from * to * around, except omit the last 2 sc, end with sl st in the beginning sc, fasten off.

Waistband

Refer to Skirt 101 (page 129) for drawstring or elastic waist options. Make waistband desired in the same way, using 80 (88, 96, 104, 112, 120) stitches of the foundation chain.

Weave in ends, block skirt.

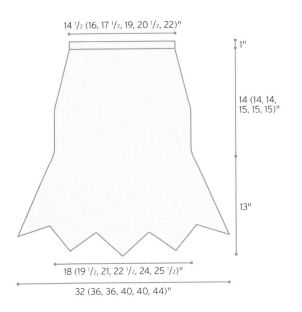

14 ¹/₂ (16, 17 ¹/₂, 19, 20 ¹/₂, 22)"

1"

14 (14, 14, 15, 15, 15)"

13"

18 (19 ¹/₂, 21, 22 ¹/₂, 24, 25 ¹/₂)"

32 (36, 36, 40, 40, 44)"

Garment 101

The Cake

THE PREVIOUS DESIGN CHAPTERS IN THIS BOOK HOLD ALL THE excitement of new ways to look at lace techniques; that was the good stuff. If you're my kind of reader, you won't be here at this chapter until you absolutely have to read these instructions in order to start crocheting. I can live with that.

The mechanics of shaping alternate stitch techniques, fancy lace patterns, and doilies into complete garments with patterning for XS to 3XL are enormously complicated, torturous to write, and more torturous for crocheters to follow. I'd much rather use that good stuff as the frosting on a great cake; namely, a basic, classic garment that fits perfectly, made in a small repeating stitch pattern.

But this is no plain, ordinary cake. Jacket 101 and its corollary, Skirt 101, are pieces that can stand alone without the doodads. They're infinitely adaptable and wonderfully versatile patterns that you will turn to when you want to play with crochet clothes.

The Jadzia Jacket (page 28), Kylara Vest (page 44), Ming Jacket (page 110), and the skirts—Rohise (page 41), River Song (page 80), and Ping (page 116)—are examples of what you can do with these templates, using the techniques you've practiced. Take these patterns apart and you'll see that, with imagination and a bit of calculating, the lace parts can be swapped out for just about anything you want to try. So let's have some cake, huh?

JACKET 101

• •• ◆ •• •

OF ALL THE TOPS I HAVE EVER CROCHETED, KNITTED, SEWN (YES, SEWN!), AND DESIGNED, THIS CONFIGURATION IS MY FAVORITE. IT FEATURES MY USUAL M.O. OF RELAXED GAUGE, LACE STITCH PATTERN, AND SEAMLESS TOP-DOWN CONSTRUCTION. THE V-NECK, OPEN FRONT, BODY-SKIMMING STYLING IS VERSATILE AND ATTRACTIVE ON ALL FIGURES. ALMOST EVERYTHING ELSE ABOUT IT IS ADJUSTABLE, AND TWEAKABLE, SO YOU WILL BE EMPOWERED TO CREATE A CROCHETED WEARABLE THAT IS MADE TO MEASURE, FITTED, AND FINISHED PERFECTLY FOR YOUR PERSONAL SHAPE.

TO PROVIDE A BASIC TEMPLATE AND A CANVAS FOR YOUR OWN EXPERIMENTATION, I AM SHOWING THIS JACKET AS A CLOSE-FITTING GARMENT WITH THREE-QUARTER-LENGTH SLEEVES. SEE THE DESIGN KYLARA VEST (PAGE 44) FOR FASHIONING A TRUE SLEEVELESS VERSION.

THE DESIGN IS RATED "EXPERIENCED" DUE TO THE COMPLEXITY OF THE SHAPING, THE CONVOLUTED PATTERNING, AND THE SELF-KNOWLEDGE REQUIRED TO DO PERSONAL FITTING. BUT THIS DOES NOT MEAN THAT BEGINNING OR INTERMEDIATE CROCHETERS WITH A SOLID GRASP OF BASIC STITCHES AND SKILLS SHOULDN'T ATTEMPT A JACKET LIKE THIS. HOW ELSE DOES ONE BECOME "EXPERIENCED," AFTER ALL?

SKILL LEVEL: EXPERIENCED ◆ ◆ ◆ ◆

SIZES
XS (S, M, L, XL, 2XL, 3XL); finished bust 33 (36, 39, 42, 45, 48, 51)" (84 [91, 99, 106.5, 114, 122, 129.5]cm) to fit body bust up to 34 (37, 40, 43, 46, 49, 52)" (86 [94, 101.5, 109, 117, 124.5, 132] cm) with a bit of negative ease

MATERIALS
See the individual designs for specific materials and amounts. Here are some pointers to get you started.

SUGGESTED YARN DK weight, ranging from heavy sportweight to light worsted weight. Generally the knitting gauge for this range of yarns will be around 5 to 5.5 stitches to the inch (2.5cm) on a size 6 (4mm) to 7 (4.5mm)

knitting needle. Yarns in this range may have from 100 to 120 yards (91–110m) to the 1.75 oz (50g) ball, but this will vary greatly depending on the density of the fiber. Feel free to try any yarn or combination of yarns that gives you the stated crocheted gauge.

SUGGESTED HOOK To keep the fabric open and pliable with good drape, use a larger hook than traditional sense might dictate. I like to go up two or even three hook sizes from the suggested knitting needle size. For DK-weight yarn, that means starting with an H-8 (5mm) to I-9 (5.5mm) crochet hook, changing hooks until you are pleased with the resulting fabric.

GAUGE (APPROXIMATE, AS CROCHETED)
11 Fsc or sc = 4" (10cm)

In shell stitch pattern, 2 repeats of (shell, sc) = 3" (7.5cm), 4 rows = 2¼" (5.5cm) (will lengthen with blocking to 2½" [6.5cm] or more)

STITCHES USED
Fsc (see page 134 for technique), sl st, ch, sc, dc

STITCH DEFINITIONS
SH (SHELL) (dc, ch 1, dc, ch 1, dc) all in the same stitch or space.

INC-SH (INCREASE SHELL) (dc, ch 1, dc, ch 1, dc, ch 1, dc) all in the same stitch or space.

Basic Shell Stitch Pattern (in rows)

—To work even, without increase or decrease, repeat these two rows for Basic Shell Stitch Pattern:

PATT A Ch 1, sc in the first dc, [SH in the next sc, sc in the 2nd dc of the next shell] across, end with sc in the 3rd ch of tch, turn.

PATT B Ch 4 (counts as dc, ch 1), dc in the first sc, [sc in the 2nd dc of the next shell, SH in the next sc] across, except omit the last SH, instead end with (dc, ch 1, dc) in the last sc, turn.

—To increase at the ends of a row after a Patt A:

PATT C Ch 4, (dc, ch 1, dc) for a shell in the first sc, [sc in the 2nd dc of the next shell, SH in the next sc] across, end with SH in the last sc, turn—shells at each end.

—To work even at ends of a row after a Patt C:

PATT D Ch 4, dc in the first dc of the beginning shell, sc in the 2nd dc of the beginning shell, [SH in the next sc, sc in the 2nd dc of the next shell] across to the ending shell, over the ending shell make sc in the 2nd dc, (dc, ch 1, dc) in the 3rd ch of tch, turn—half-shells at each end.

—To increase at the ends of a row after a Patt C:

PATT E Ch 4, (dc, ch 1, dc) for shell in the first dc, sc in the 2nd dc of the beginning shell, [SH in the next sc, sc in the 2nd dc of the next shell] across to the ending shell, over the ending shell make sc in the 2nd dc, SH in the 3rd ch of tch, turn—shells at each end.

Here are rows to use for making increases for raglan-type shoulders in a yoke or for a hip flare.

—To increase at four corners or points after working even (there is a sc in each corner):

PATT F Begin the row as instructed, *work in shell stitch pattern as established to the next corner sc or marker point, make INC-SH in the corner sc*; repeat from * to * 3 times, end the row as instructed.

—To increase at four corners after a Patt F (there is an increase shell in each corner):

PATT G Begin the row as instructed, *work in shell stitch pattern as established to the next increase shell, over the increase shell work [sc in the first ch-1 sp, INC-SH in the next ch-1 sp, sc in the next ch-1 sp]*; repeat from * to * 3 times, end the row as instructed.

—To work even at four corners after a Patt F or Patt G (there is an increase shell in each corner):

PATT B   PATT A

BASIC SHELL STITCH PATTERNS IN ROWS

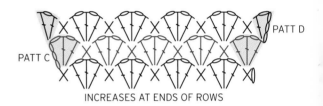

PATT C   PATT D

INCREASES AT ENDS OF ROWS

PATT E

INCREASES AT ENDS OF ROWS

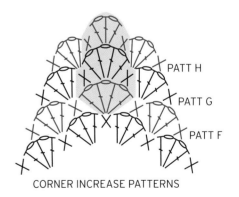

PATT H   PATT G   PATT F

CORNER INCREASE PATTERNS

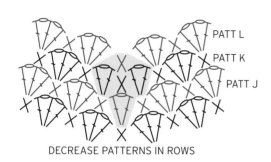

DECREASE PATTERNS IN ROWS

BASIC SHELL STITCH PATTERNS IN RNDS

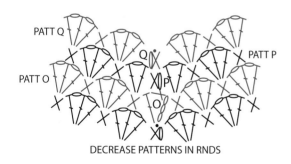

DECREASE PATTERNS IN RNDS

PATT H Begin the row as instructed, *work in shell stitch pattern as established to the next increase shell, over the increase shell work [sc in the first ch-1 sp, SH in the next ch-1 sp, sc in the next ch-1 sp]*; repeat from * to * 3 times, end the row as instructed.

—To decrease at four points, as for a waist nip, use these three rows.

There must be a sc at each of the points in order to start. Mark the stitch at the center of each of the four points and move or wrap the marker up as you go.

PATT J Begin the row as instructed, *work in shell stitch pattern as established to the next point marker, instead of SH make (dc, ch 1, dc) in marked sc*; repeat from * to * 3 times, end the row as instructed.

PATT K Begin the row as instructed, *work in shell stitch pattern as established to the sc before the next point marker, instead of SH make (dc, ch 1, dc) in the sc before the marker, sc in the ch-1 sp at the marker, (dc, ch 1, dc) in the sc after the marker*; repeat from * to * 3 times, end the row as instructed.

PATT L Begin the row as instructed, *work in shell stitch pattern as established to the sc before the next point marker, SH in the sc before the marker, skip the next (dc, ch 1, dc), sc in the marked point sc, skip the next (dc, ch 1, dc), SH in the next sc after the marker*; repeat from * to * 3 times, end the row as instructed.

Basic Shell Stitch Pattern (in rounds) for sleeves or for skirt

—To work even without increase or decrease, repeat these two rounds for basic shell stitch pattern:

PATT M Ch 1, sc in the next dc, [SH in the next sc, sc in the 2nd dc of the next shell] around, except omit the last sc, instead end with sl st in the beginning sc, turn.

PATT N Ch 3 (counts as dc), [sc in the 2nd dc of the next shell, SH in the next sc] around, except omit the last SH, instead complete the beginning shell with (dc, ch 1, dc) in the same sc as at the beginning, sc in third ch of the beginning ch, turn.

—To decrease at the underside of the arm for a sleeve taper after a Patt M, use these three rounds:

PATT O Ch 3, [sc in the 2nd dc of the next shell, SH in the next sc] around, except omit the last SH, instead end with dc in the same sc as at the beginning, sc in the top of tch to complete a half-shell, turn.

PATT P Ch 1, sc in the beginning ch-sp, (dc, ch 1, dc) for a half-shell in the next sc, [sc in the 2nd dc of the next shell, SH in the next sc] around, except in the last sc make (dc, ch 1, dc) for a half-shell, sl st in the beginning sc, turn.

PATT Q Ch 1, sc in the same sc, skip the half-shell, [SH in the next sc, sc in the 2nd dc of the next shell] around, except skip the half-shell, end with sl st in the beginning sc, turn.

INSTRUCTIONS
Yoke

The yoke is a shaped section that forms the neckline and shoulders of the jacket and is the most critical (and most complicated) piece of the puzzle. Once you have slogged through the yoke, you're basically home free.

Fsc 25 (25, 25, 25, 29, 29, 29) to measure approximately 9 (9, 9, 9, 10½, 10½, 10½)" (23 [23, 23, 23, 26.5, 26.5, 26.5]cm) slightly stretched, turn the foundation so the sc edge is on top and begin work across the sc edge. Mark the middle stitch at each of the four principal corners and move or wrap markers up as you go.

Size XS

ROW 1 Ch 4, SH in the first sc for the beginning increase shell, *skip the next sc, sc in the next sc, skip the next sc, INC-SH in the next sc*, [skip the next sc, sc in the next sc, skip the next sc, SH in the next sc] 3 times, repeat from * to * twice, turn—7 shells.

ROW 2 Ch 4, over the beginning increase shell work (dc in the first dc, sc in the next ch-1 sp, INC-SH in the next ch-1 sp, sc in the next ch-1 sp), SH in the next sc, *over the increase shell work (sc in the first ch-1 sp, INC-SH in the next ch-1 sp, sc in the next ch-1 sp), SH in the next sc*, [sc in the 2nd dc of the next shell, SH in the next sc] 3 times, repeat from * to * twice, except omit the last SH, instead end with (dc, ch 1, dc) in the 3rd ch of tch, turn—10 shells plus half-shells at ends.

ROW 3 Begin as Patt A; increase corners as Patt G; end as Patt A—15 shells.

ROW 4 Begin with an increase as Patt C; increase corners as Patt G; end with an increase as Patt C—20 shells.

ROW 5 Begin as Patt D; work even corners as Patt H; end as Patt D—23 shells plus half-shells at ends.

ROW 6 Work Patt A—24 shells.

ROW 7 Begin with an increase as Patt C; increase corners as Patt F; end with an increase as Patt C—25 shells.

ROW 8–11 Repeat Rows 5–7, then Row 5 once more—33 shells plus half-shells at ends.

Size S

ROWS 1–4 Same as size XS Rows 1–4.

ROW 5 Begin as Patt D; increase corners as Patt G; end as Patt D—23 shells plus half-shells at ends.

ROW 6 Begin as Patt A; work even corners as Patt H; end as Patt A—28 shells.

ROW 7 Work Patt C—29 shells.

ROW 8 Begin as Patt D; increase corners as Patt F; end as Patt D.

ROW 9–12 Repeat Rows 6–8, then Row 6 once more—38 shells.

Size M

This size begins with an extra increase at center back.

ROW 1 Ch 4, SH in the first sc for the beginning increase shell, *skip the next sc, sc in the next sc, skip the next sc, INC-SH in the next sc*, [skip the next sc, sc in the next sc, skip the next sc, SH in the next sc]; repeat from * to * once; repeat between [ ] once; repeat from * to * twice, turn—7 shells.

ROW 2 Ch 4, over the beginning increase shell work (dc in the first dc, sc in the next ch-1 sp, INC-SH in the next ch-1 sp, sc in the next ch-1 sp), SH in the next sc, *over the next increase shell work (sc in the first ch-1 sp, INC-SH in the next ch-1 sp, sc in the next ch-1 sp), SH in the next sc*, [sc in the 2nd dc of the next shell, SH in the next sc], over the center back increase shell work (sc in the first ch-1 sp, SH in the next ch-1 sp, sc in the next ch-1 sp), SH in the next sc; repeat between [ ] once, repeat from * to * twice, except omit the last SH, instead end with (dc, ch 1, dc) in the 3rd ch of tch, turn—11 shells plus half-shells at ends.

Discontinue shaping at center back, continue with four principal corners.

ROW 3–12 Same as size S Rows 3–12 with one extra shell in each row—39 shells.

Size L

This size begins with an extra increase at center back.

ROWS 1–2 Same as size M Rows 1–2.

Discontinue shaping at center back, continue with four principal corners.

ROW 3 Begin as Patt A; increase corners as Patt G; end as Patt A—16 shells.

ROW 4 Begin with an increase as Patt C; increase corners as Patt G; end with an increase as Patt C—21 shells.

ROW 5 Begin as Patt D; increase corners as Patt G; end as Patt D—24 shells plus half-shells at ends.

ROW 6 Begin as Patt A; increase corners as Patt G; end as Patt A—29 shells.

ROW 7 Begin with an increase as Patt C; work even corners as Patt H; end with an increase as Patt C—34 shells.

ROW 8 Work Patt D—33 shells plus half-shells at ends.

ROW 9 Begin as Patt A; increase corners as Patt F; end as Patt A—34 shells.

ROWS 10–13 Repeat Rows 7–9, then Row 7 once more—44 shells.

Size XL

ROW 1 Ch 4, SH in the first sc for the beginning increase shell, *skip the next sc, sc in the next sc, skip the next sc, INC-SH in the next sc*, [skip the next sc, sc in the next sc, skip the next sc, SH in the next sc] 4 times, repeat from * to * twice, turn—8 shells.

This size requires an extra increase at center back.

ROW 2 Ch 4, over the beginning increase shell work (dc in the first dc, sc in the next ch-1 sp, INC-SH in the next ch-1 sp, sc in the next ch-1 sp), SH in the next sc, *over the next increase shell work (sc in the first ch-1 sp, INC-SH in the next ch-1 sp, sc in the next ch-1 sp)*, [SH in the next sc, sc in the 2nd dc of the next shell] twice, INC-SH in the next sc, [sc in the 2nd dc of the next shell, SH in the next sc] twice, repeat from * to * once, SH in the next sc, repeat from * to * once, end with (dc, ch 1, dc) in the 3rd ch of tch, turn—11 shells plus half-shells at ends.

ROW 3 Ch 1, sc in the first dc, SH in the next sc, *over the next increase shell work (sc in the first ch-1 sp, INC-SH in the next ch-1 sp, sc in the next ch-1 sp), SH in the next sc*, [sc in the 2nd dc of the next shell, SH in the next sc]; repeat from * to * once, repeat between [ ] twice; over the center back increase shell work (sc in the first ch-1 sp, SH in the next ch-1 sp, sc in the next ch-1 sp), SH in the next sc, repeat between [ ] twice; repeat from * to * once; repeat between [ ] once; repeat from * to * once, end with sc in the 3rd ch of tch, turn—17 shells.

Discontinue shaping at center back, continue with four principal corners.

ROW 4 Begin with an increase as Patt C; increase corners as Patt G; end with an increase as Patt C—22 shells.

ROW 5 Begin as Patt D; increase corners as Patt G; end as Patt D—25 shells plus half-shells at ends.

ROW 6 Begin as Patt A; increase corners as Patt G; end as Patt A—30 shells.

ROW 7 Begin with an increase as Patt C; work even corners as Patt H; end with an increase as Patt C—35 shells.

ROW 8 Work Patt D—34 shells plus half-shells at ends.

ROW 9 Begin as Patt A; increase corners as Patt F; end as Patt A—35 shells.

ROWS 10–13 Repeat Rows 7–9, then Row 7 once more—45 shells.

Sizes 2XL (3XL)

ROWS 1–6 Same as size XL Rows 1–6—31 shells.

ROW 7 Begin with an increase as Patt C; increase corners as Patt G; end with an increase as Patt C—36 shells.

ROW 8 Begin as Patt D; work even corners as Patt H; end as Patt D—39 shells plus half-shells at ends.

ROW 9 Work Patt A—40 shells.

ROW 10 Begin with an increase as Patt C; increase corners as Patt F; end with an increase as Patt C—41 shells.

ROWS 11–14 Repeat Rows 8–10, then Row 8 once more—48 shells plus half-shells at ends.

Fit Tip

Even though this is a close-fitting design, the armholes may seem as if they're going to be too small at this stage. Bear in mind that finishing with sleeves and blocking will stretch out the "raglan" lines formed by the shaping at the four corners and the underarm will drop considerably. Adding rows here will result in a longer yoke and sleeve "cap," but will not alter the number of stitches in the armhole, so the sleeve circumference will remain the same.

If you are certain you will need a deeper yoke and armhole for your size, you can add approximately 1" (2.5cm) in length by inserting two rows before joining the underarms, as long as you end with a shell at each of the four corners. Sizes XS, S, and L may simply repeat working even rows; sizes M, XL, 2XL, and 3XL must complete the V-neck shaping in the course of any additional rows.

Body

Sizes XS, S, and L have completed the front V-neck shaping; size M completes it in the next row; sizes XL, 2XL, and 3XL will finish a row later. All sizes have a shell at the middle of each of the four principal corners. Join the fronts and back with additional stitches at each underarm to make one continuous row.

ROW 1 (JOIN UNDERARMS) Begin as Patt A (B, C, D, D, A, A), *work in shell stitch pattern as established to the next corner shell, sc in the 2nd dc of the corner shell, ch 1, Fsc 5 (5, 5, 5, 5, 5, 11) for the underarm, skip the next 6 (7, 7, 8, 8, 9, 9) shells for the armhole, sc in the 2nd dc of the next corner shell*; repeat from * to * once, work in shell stitch pattern as established, end as Patt A (B, C, D, D, A, A).

All Sizes Except 3XL

ROW 2 Begin as Patt B (A, D, A, A, C), *work in shell stitch pattern as established, making SH in the sc before the underarm, skip the first 2 sc of the underarm, sc in the next sc, skip the remaining 2 sc of the underarm, SH in the next sc after the underarm*; repeat from * to * once across the other underarm, work in shell stitch pattern as established, end as Patt B (A, D, A, A, C)—21 shells plus half-shells at ends (24 shells, 25 shells plus half-shells at ends, 28 shells, 29 shells, 32 shells).

Size 3XL

ROW 2 Begin as Patt C, work the same as for the other sizes, except at the underarms (skip the first 2 sc of the underarm, sc in the next sc, skip the next 2 sc, SH in the next sc, skip the next 2 sc, sc in the next sc, skip the remaining 2 sc), end as Patt C—34 shells.

Fit Tip

If you are inserting bust shaping, please read the section that follows to decide where to place the wedge before continuing.

All Sizes

ROW 3 Work as Patt A (B, A, B, C, D, D).
ROW 4 Work as Patt B (A, B, A, D, A, A).
ROW 5 Work as Patt A (B, A, B, A, B, B)—22 shells (23 shells plus half-shells at ends, 26 shells, 27 shells plus half-shells at ends, 30 shells, 31 shells plus half-shells at ends, 33 shells plus half-shells at ends).

The Wedge: Bust Shaping (optional)

If you'd like to insert wedges (short-row shaping) in the jacket fronts to accommodate a full bust, here are my suggestions. Put the wedges where you need the extra fabric, more or less centered on the fullest part of your bust, somewhere between Row 2 and Row 5 of the body. Wedges go from the front edge past the fullness of the bust, but not quite all the way to the center of the underarm.

First Side

Begin the row as you would the next row in the pattern, work in shell stitch pattern as established, stopping with (SH in the next sc) a couple of inches (several cm) (one, one and a half, or even two shells) before you reach the center of the next underarm, sl st in the 2nd dc of the next shell, turn. Sl st in the first dc of the shell, sl st in the next ch-1 sp, sl st in the 2nd dc of the shell, SH in the next sc, work in shell stitch pattern as established, ending the row as the next row in pattern. Put the last loop on hold.

Second Side

At the other front, locate the shell past the center of the other underarm that corresponds to the place where you turned the first wedge. Join yarn with sl st in the 2nd dc of that shell, SH in the next sc, work in shell stitch pattern as established to the end of the front edge, turn. Begin as the next row in pattern, work in shell stitch pattern as established, stopping with SH in the last sc of the short row, sl st in the 2nd dc of the last shell of the short row, fasten off.

Return to the other front edge, replace the loop on the hook, and continue with body rows, ignoring the slip stitches and working the repeats as they face you.

For Ming jacket, stop the body here and continue with the Lace Border (page 112).

Body Continued

The shell stitch fabric has quite a bit of stretch and tends to widen where you are wider and skinny out (draw narrower and longer) where you are smaller. So if you continue to crochet the body straight-sided, without shaping, this close-fitting design will give the appearance of a slightly tapered waist and a slightly flared hip. But for a true fitted body, here are suggestions for a waist "nip" and a hip "flare."

The Nip and the Flare

For the most balanced, smoothest appearance, I use a four-point nip/flare; shaping at four places more or less evenly spaced around the body, two centered at either side of the front and two in the back. At this gauge, done just once, it will decrease/increase the body by four shell stitch pattern repeats, approximately 6" (15cm) in circumference.

Fit Tip

If you are aiming for a more dramatic nip or flare you can certainly make more than four points around, or repeat the set of decrease/increase rows and shape once more at the same four points. But be advised that extreme shaping of the fabric may cause puckering or ballooning, which appears as a "bloused" effect in a top or a "dirndl" effect in a skirt, instead of a subtle, smooth, clean taper.

The spacing of the nip/flare is a matter of taste. I try to avoid placing a line of shaping directly under the point of the bust, but, again, this is up to you. The distance between the two front points and between the two back points should be similar, but does not have to be exactly the same.

You can start the nip at any row in the body once you have joined the fronts and back at the underarms, but generally you should at least work the body until it is past the fullest part of the bust. That could be from one to four or five inches (2.5–12.5cm) below the underarm. After the stitches are locked into place with blocking, it will take a row or two of working even below the nip before the fabric reaches its narrowest. So don't wait too long before the level of your waist or your narrowest body spot to start your nip or you'll miss the target.

Similarly, the flare will not reach its widest until a row or two after the set of increases, so start it somewhere below the waist but above the fullest part of your hip.

There is enough stretch and natural expansion in the bottom edge of shell stitch fabric that you might not need to create more top-of-hip room for a short or cropped jacket. But for a longer garment that skims the hip, you'll appreciate the flare, which can be used to put back the width taken away by the nip (plus more, if needed) or to create hip shaping in a skirt.

The Jadzia Jacket (page 28) offers specific instructions for making a fit-and-flatter jacket with Broomstick lace trim. But as a general plan for getting started, locate and mark four points at four sc spaced around the body as outlined above; move or wrap markers up into the center of the stitches in the following rows until all your shaping is completed.

The Nip

Work [Patt J, Patt K, Patt L], then continue the body working even to length desired.

The flare uses the exact same increasing technique as yoke shaping. Either continue with the same four points as marked for a previous nip, or locate and mark four sc points as outlined above. Skirt 101 (page 129) employs a four-point flare in the round to shape the yoke of a skirt that is the basis for Rohise (page 41), River Song (page 80), and Ping (page 116).

The Flare

Work [Patt F, Patt H], then continue working even to the length desired.

Sleeves

Fit Tip

This is a three-quarter-length sleeve, approximately 10" (25.5cm) long before edging or trim. For a nearly sleeveless "cap" shoulder, omit the sleeves entirely and finish the armholes with edging. For shorter sleeves, you may stop crocheting anywhere during the following rows and finish as desired.

To lengthen the sleeve or for long sleeves, decide where you want the length: at the top of the arm where the sleeve is fullest, between the sets of taper rounds to evenly distribute the length, or at the bottom of the sleeve where it is narrowest. Add pairs of rounds in pattern after completing a Patt M, alternating [Patt N, Patt M] as desired, making sure you end ready for the following round.

Sleeves are worked onto the armholes back and forth in joined rounds using (Patts M, N, O, P, and Q), tapering the sleeves by making decreases 2 (2, 2, 2, 3, 3) times. Begin working in the opposite direction of the armhole shell stitch pattern in the middle ch of one underarm foundation.

All Sizes Except 3XL

RND 1 Join with sl st in the 3rd ch of the underarm foundation, ch 3, skip the next 2 ch of the foundation, sc in the next sc row edge after the underarm, work in shell stitch pattern as established around the armhole, ending with sc in the next sc row edge before the underarm, skip the next 2 ch of the foundation, (dc, ch 1 dc) in the same ch as at the beginning, sc in top of the beginning ch, turn—8 (9, 9, 10, 10, 11) shells.

Size 3XL

RND 1 Join with sl st in 6th ch of the underarm foundation, ch 1, sc in the same ch, skip the next 2 ch, SH in the next ch, skip the next 2 ch, sc in the next sc row edge after the underarm, work in shell stitch pattern as established around the armhole, ending with sc in the next sc row edge before the underarm, skip the next 2 ch of the foundation, SH in the next ch, skip the remaining 2 ch, sl st in the beginning sc, turn—12 shells.

Sizes XS (S, M, L, XL)

RNDS 2–6 Work sleeve rounds [Patt M, Patt N] for 2 times, then Patt M once more—8 (9, 9, 10, 10) shells.
RNDS 7–11 Work sleeve taper rounds [Patt O, Patt P, Patt Q], then work even round Patt N, then Patt M—7 (8, 8, 9, 9) shells.
RNDS 12–16 Repeat Rnds 7–11—6 (7, 7, 8, 8) shells.

Size 2XL

RND 2 Work sleeve round Patt M—11 shells.
RNDS 3–7 Work sleeve taper rounds [Patt O, Patt P, Patt Q], then work even round Patt N, then Patt M—10 shells.
RNDS 8–16 Repeat Rnds 3–7, then Rnds 3–6 once more—8 shells.

Size 3XL

RND 2–6 Work sleeve taper rounds [Patt O, Patt P, Patt Q], then work even round Patt N, then Patt M—11 shells.
RNDS 7–16 Repeat Rnds 2–6 for 2 times—9 shells.
For Ming Jacket, stop each sleeve here and continue with mesh trim (page 114).
Make sleeve on the other armhole in the same way.

Finishing

There are all the ways in the universe to finish, edge, trim, and otherwise embellish this basic jacket. Or not. Although it is possible to launch immediately into a different stitch pattern, lace trim, or edging, I like having a nice, neat, even row of plain stitches as a jumping-off base.

Bottom Edges

The bottoms of this jacket body and sleeves end in shell stitch pattern. To make these edges ready for the next stage, you may wish to convert the shell stitch pattern into a plain solid stitch pattern. Here are my suggestions for a simple sc edging that works well as a foundation row for anything else you might want to try.

To hold in the edge and tame the natural expansion of the shells, either make a row of sc in a firmer gauge by switching to a smaller hook, or create fewer sc across each shell stitch repeat, or do both.

FIRM EDGE Ch 1, sc in the same st, make 5 sc across each shell stitch repeat by [sc in each dc and ch-1 sp, skip each sc].

For an edge that maintains the same width as the fabric, neither pulling in nor stretching out the shell stitches, use the same-size hook as you used for the body of the jacket and make it the same way as the firm edge above, keeping the sc to the same gauge as the body.

To allow for bottom expansion or to emphasize the lower flare that occurs with shell stitch fabric, make a greater number of sc across each repeat or switch to a larger hook, or both.

FLARED EDGE Ch 1, sc in the same st, make 6 sc across each shell stitch repeat by [sc in each dc, ch-1 sp and sc].

Front and Neck Edges

Finishing raw edges is one of my least favorite crochet tasks. The front edges of this type of design can't stand alone, are often messy or difficult to read and count. Working over your row edges evenly with sc gives a much more finished look, prepares the jacket for a band or trim, and helps your front edges keep their shape.

The rows of shell stitch pattern in this jacket will grow in length as the shells and stitches lock into place and bloom with blocking. Your edging has to be just as flexible in order to go with the flow, so making it just right can be tricky. You don't want this sc edge to be so firm that it pulls up the fronts, nor do you want a sloppy, saggy finish. Three factors can make or break a clean edge: the number of stitches, where you place the stitches, and the gauge.

1. HOW MANY? Crocheting sc evenly across row edges sometimes means putting extra sc here and there, adjusting the count as you go. But for general purposes I like to make the same number of sc in each type of stitch, keeping things simple.

FRONT EDGES Usually I make one sc in each sc row edge, 2 sc in each dc row edge. You will have to really look at the ends of the rows to see the progression of sc/dc, but whatever number you crochet along one front, make sure you crochet the same number along the other front. Occasionally, I will put an extra sc in the dc row edge at the base of the V-neck shaping to help the curve lie flat. Often the band or lace or trim you want to apply next requires a specific stitch count and you have to adjust the numbers. Try to add/omit sc as evenly as possible around the edge for the best appearance.

BACK NECK EDGE This is a piece of cake because of the Fsc at the back neck. Make one sc in each ch of the foundation.

2. WHERE? You can make sc edging by inserting the hook under all strands of the stem of the last stitch in the row, into the big space, around the whole row edge stitch. This creates gaps between the edging and the fabric of the fronts, which is great when you want to maintain and emphasize the laciness or leave yourself some instant buttonholes. For a more delicate, tighter finish, especially if your yarn is thicker, make the sc edging into the stitches of the row edge instead of around them. In other words, insert the hook into a sc row edge, under two strands of the stem of the sc, and make one sc. On a dc row edge, insert the hook under two strands of the edge, make a sc, insert the hook under two strands further down the same dc row edge, make a sc. Pay attention to the strands you're going into and try to do it the same way for each dc row edge.

When making sc along the chains of the back neck foundation, you also have choices. I advise inserting the hook under all top loops of each foundation stitch (the two top strands and the funny one that runs across the stem). This way you are putting sc into the same place as the first row of stitch pattern in the yoke, minimizing any sagging that might occur. But you may choose to go under just two or under only one strand of the foundation chain each time. In any case, do them all the same way.

3. HOW TIGHT? The gauge is always the most difficult aspect to describe and to do. Even when I put just the right number of sc in exactly the same places each time, I routinely rip and recrochet my sc edges in order to make them attractive because my gauge is all over the place. It takes experience to make a row of sc in an even gauge that does not pucker or ruffle.

Fit Tip

One reason you might want to make a firmer sc edge is to fix a neckline that is too loose. To firm up or close up a back neck that is way too wide, make the sc along the foundation chains of the neck in a tighter gauge by crocheting more firmly or switching to a smaller hook.

SKIRT 101

THE BEAUTY OF A PULL-ON SKIRT IS THAT YOU CAN DISPENSE WITH THE FUSSY FITTING AND SEAMING. THE STANDARD DIFFERENCE BETWEEN WAIST AND HIP CIRCUMFERENCES FOR WOMEN IS AROUND TEN INCHES (25.5cm), HOWEVER NOT ALL BODIES ARE STANDARD. A DRAWSTRING OR ELASTIC WAIST ALLOWS FOR A FORGIVING, ADJUSTABLE FIT. THE TRICK IS ENGINEERING A SKIRT THAT WILL PULL ON WITHOUT LEAVING TOO MUCH FABRIC TO BE EVENTUALLY GATHERED AROUND THE WAIST.

The aim is to create crocheted fabric with enough give. Lace stitch patterns, particularly shell stitches, when worked in a relaxed gauge, in themselves provide enormous stretch. But the real trick to this design is the foundation single crochet (Fsc). This technique makes a row of foundation chains and a beginning row of single crochets in one. The resulting foundation is both sturdy and elastic, with stitches that are easy to count and easy to work into. I totally expect this skirt waistband to stretch six inches (15cm) or more. That means it is possible to start with a waist that is approximately halfway between your waist and hip measurements. From there you can increase to full hip circumference for a slim-fitting skirt body with a slightly tapered waist.

Finding a good fit requires choosing the correct size to crochet. That means a bit (okay, it means a lot) of experimentation, sometimes referred to as swatching, but not the usual kind of swatching. Once you have settled on the specific skirt design and are reasonably certain your yarn is within the recommended range, choose the size that gives you a finished full hip measurement closest to your actual hip, with an inch (2.5cm) either way.

*Go ahead and do the Fsc and work at least four rounds of shell stitch pattern. Give the piece a good tug in all directions and measure the gauge; most important, the stitch gauge. If you are hitting the stitch gauge (width), that's good enough; worry about the row gauge (length) later. Try it on. If you absolutely cannot shimmy into the waist, then start over. The best fix would be to make the same size but crochet the Fsc a touch more relaxed by using a larger hook just for the Fsc. You could also move to the next larger skirt size, but be advised that you'll be jumping up in hip circumference as well. Repeat from * until you are satisfied.

Keep trying on your skirt as you work. It's useful to have a finished waistband to give you a more accurate feel for the skirt length. A logical place to stop the body is just after the increases for the hip, or alternately when the first or second ball of yarn runs out. Skip ahead and make the drawstring option with the string or the waistband for elastic, but hold off on the inside casing and elastic.

SKILL LEVEL: INTERMEDIATE ✦ ✦ ✦ ✦

SIZES

XS (S, M, L, XL, 2XL, 3XL); finished waistband 29 (32, 35, 38, 41, 44, 47)" (74 [81, 89, 96.5, 104, 112, 119]cm); finished full hip 36 (39, 42, 45, 48, 51, 54)" (91 [99, 106.5, 114, 122, 137]cm) to fit body hip up to 35 (38, 41, 44, 47, 50, 53)" (89 [96.5, 104, 112, 119, 127, 134.5]cm) with plenty of stretch to fit

MATERIALS

See individual designs for specific yarn, amounts and tools.

FOR ELASTIC CASING OPTION

Sturdy matching thread, waistband elastic, ¾" to 1" (2–2.5cm) wide, cut to measure

FOR NO-SEW ELASTIC OPTION ⅛" (3mm) narrow braided or round elastic, cut to measure

GAUGE (AS CROCHETED)

This is a guideline gauge for some of the patterns in the previous chapters that are crocheted in midweight yarn (anywhere from heavy sport to DK to light worsted) using an I-9 (5.5mm) hook.

11 Fsc or sc = 4" (10cm)

In Basic Shell Stitch Pattern, (shell, sc) 2 times = 3" (7.5cm); 4 rounds = 2¼" (5.5cm) and will surely lengthen with blocking to 4 rounds = 2½" (6.5cm) or even more

STITCHES USED

Fsc (see page 134 for technique), sl st, ch, sc, dc, rev sc

STITCH DEFINITIONS

SH (SHELL) (dc, ch 1, dc, ch 1, dc) all in the same stitch or space.

INC-SH (INCREASE SHELL) (dc, ch 1, dc, ch 1, dc, ch 1, dc) all in the same stitch or space.

For Basic Shell Stitch Pattern and shaping in rounds, and for stitch diagrams, see explanations in Jacket 101 (page 120).

INSTRUCTIONS

Skirt Yoke

This is the skirt yoke used for Rohise (page 41), River Song (page 80), and Ping (page 116), finished to different lengths according to the individual patterns.

Rounds begin at center back. Fsc 80 (88, 96, 104, 112, 120, 128) to measure approx 29 (32, 35, 38, 41, 44, 47)" (74 [81, 89, 96.5, 104, 112, 119]cm), turn the foundation so the sc edge is on top, sl st in the beginning sc to form a ring, careful not to twist foundation, begin work across the sc edge.

RND 1 Ch 1, sc in the same sc, [skip the next sc, SH in the next sc, skip the next sc, sc in the next sc] 20 (22, 24, 26, 28, 30, 32) times, except omit the last sc, instead end with sl st in the beginning sc, turn—20 (22, 24, 26, 28, 30, 32) shells.

Sizes XS (S, M)

RNDS 2–6 Work Patt N, then [Patt M, Patt N] 2 times.

Sizes L (XL, 2XL)

RNDS 2–7 Work Patt N, then [Patt M, Patt N] 2 times, then Patt M once more.

Size 3XL

RNDS 2–8 Work Patt N, then [Patt M, Patt N] 3 times.

The Flare: Hip Shaping

As introduced in Jacket 101 (page 120), hip shaping for a skirt is done in a similar way to yoke shaping in a top. The flare is a set of four increase points evenly spaced around the skirt yoke. Here are more details on how to create the specific flare for this skirt. Mark the center stitch at each of the four increase points; move or wrap markers up as you go.

Sizes XS (S, M)

RND 7 Ch 1, sc in the next dc, *[SH in the next sc, sc in the 2nd dc of the next shell] twice, INC-SH in the next sc, sc in the 2nd dc of the next shell; [SH in the next sc, sc in the 2nd dc of the next shell] 4 (5, 6) times, INC-SH in the next sc, sc in the 2nd dc of the next shell; [SH in the next sc, sc in the 2nd dc of the next shell] twice*; repeat from * to * once except omit the last sc, instead end with sl st in the beginning sc, turn.

RND 8 Ch 3, *[sc in the 2nd dc of the next shell, SH in the next sc] across to the next increase shell, over the increase shell work (sc in the first ch-1 sp, SH in the second ch-1 sp, sc in the third ch-1 sp), SH in the next sc*; repeat from * to * 3 times; sc in the 2nd dc of the next shell, SH in the next sc, sc in the 2nd dc of the next shell, end with (dc, ch 1, dc) in the same sc as at the beginning, sc in the third ch of the beginning ch, turn—24 (26, 28) shells.

Sizes L (XL, 2XL)

RND 8 Ch 3, *[sc in the 2nd dc of the next shell, SH in the next sc] twice, sc in the 2nd dc of the next shell, INC-SH in the next sc, [sc in the 2nd dc of the next shell, SH in the next sc] 6 (7, 8) times, sc in the 2nd dc of the next shell, INC-SH in the next sc, [sc in the 2nd dc of the next shell, SH in the next sc] 3 times*; repeat from * to * once, except omit the last SH, instead end with (dc, ch 1, dc) in the same sc as at the beginning, sc in the third ch of the beginning ch, turn.

RND 9 Ch 1, sc in the next dc, SH in the next sc, *[sc in the 2nd dc of the next shell, SH in the next sc] across to the next increase shell, over the increase shell work (sc in the first ch-1 sp, SH in the 2nd ch-1 sp, sc in the 3rd ch-1 sp), SH in the next sc*; repeat from * to * 3 times; [sc in the 2nd dc of the next shell, SH in the next sc] twice, end with sl st in the beginning sc, turn—30 (32, 34) shells.

Size 3XL

RND 9 Ch 1, sc in the next dc, *[SH in the next sc, sc in ͜ ͜d dc of the next shell] 3 times, INC-SH in the next sc, sc in 2nd dc of the next shell; [SH in the next sc, sc in 2nd dc of the next shell] 8 times, INC-SH in the next sc, sc in 2nd dc of the next shell; [SH in the next sc, sc in the 2nd dc of the next shell] 3 times*; repeat from * to *once, except omit the last sc, instead end with sl st in the beginning sc, turn.

RND 10 Ch 3, *[sc in the 2nd dc of the next shell, SH in the next sc] across to the next increase shell, over the increase shell work (sc in the first ch-1 sp, SH in the 2nd ch-1 sp, sc in the 3rd ch-1 sp), SH in the next sc*; repeat from * to * 3 times; [sc in the 2nd dc of the next shell, SH in the next sc] twice, sc in the 2nd dc of the next shell, end with (dc, ch 1, dc) in the same sc as at the beginning, sc in 3rd ch of the beginning ch, turn—36 shells.

Skirt Body

Sizes XS (S, M, 3XL) beginning with Patt M, sizes L (XL, 2XL) beginning with Patt N, work even across 24 (26, 28, 30, 32, 34, 36) shell repeats, alternating Patt M and Patt N until the length indicated for the specific design or for the length desired.

Fit Tip

For very full hips or to create more of an A-line shape, you may want to add another set of flares. Continue to move or wrap markers up through the center of the flare points..

To Create More Flare:

RNDS 1–3 Begin and end as the next round in pattern (either Patt M or N), work 3 rounds even, with a sc at each marker point.

RND 4 Begin and end as next round in pattern (either Patt M or N); work increases as Patt F.

RND 5 Begin and end as next round in pattern (either Patt M or N); work even across points as Patt H—adds four shell stitch repeats.

Repeat the last five rounds as desired.

Waistband Options

Drawstring Option

This option makes a narrow waistband with holes for threading a string.

With RS facing (which side is RS depends on how you ended the skirt body), with same-size hook used for Fsc, join yarn with sl st in the center back foundation ch.

RND 1 Ch 1, sc in the same ch, sc in each foundation ch around, end with sl st in the beginning sc, do not turn—80 (88, 96, 104, 112, 120, 128) sc.

RND 2 Ch 2 (counts as hdc), hdc in the same beginning sc, skip the next sc, [make a V of 2 hdc in the next sc, skip the next sc] around, end with sl st in second ch of the beginning ch, do not turn—40 (44, 48, 52, 56, 60, 64) Vs.

RND 3 Ch 1, [rev sc in the next sp between Vs, ch 1] around, end with sl st in the same sp as at the beginning, fasten off.

For a smoother edge to the waistband, omit Rnd 3. Instead, on RS, ch 1, sc in each hdc around, sl st in the beginning sc, fasten off.

String

To make a textured drawstring that has an interesting braided look, with a hook one size smaller than the one used for the skirt, begin with a slip knot, ch 2, sc in the first ch, ch 1, *without turning, insert hook from top to bottom through the front loop only of the sc just made, sc, ch 1*; repeat from * to * for the length of string desired, fasten off. Weave in ends; make a simple knot at each tip of the string. Weave the string in and out through the spaces between Vs of the waistband.

Elastic Casing Option

I prefer nonroll elastic for my skirt waists, but feel free to use any type or width of waistband elastic you like. This creates a 1" (2.5cm) wide waistband for inserting ¾" (2cm) wide elastic.

RND 1 Make this in the same way as the drawstring option above through Rnd 1, turn.

RNDS 2–5 Ch 1, sc in each sc around, sl st in the beginning sc, turn. Add or omit rounds of sc as needed for wider or narrower elastic, fasten off. Block the skirt before fitting with elastic. Cut a length of elastic to fit around your waist, plus an inch or two. Overlap the ends and temporarily safety-pin or baste the overlap to form a closed ring; you may want to adjust the elastic later. Hold the elastic to the inside of the waistband. With a blunt needle and sturdy matching thread, beginning at the inside center back, join thread securely at Rnd 1 of the waistband. Work a herringbone (backstitch) casing that forms a row of Xs between Rnd 1 and Rnd 5 (or your last round) of the waistband, enclosing the elastic. Insert the needle from right to left around the stem (front post) of the first sc of Rnd 1, moving backwards (toward the right) skip the first sc of Rnd 5, *sew around the front post of the next sc of Rnd 5, skip the next sc of Rnd 1, sew around the front post of the next sc of Rnd 1, skip the next sc of Rnd 5*; repeat from * to * around, enclosing the elastic each time, end with a stitch in the same place as at the beginning, secure the thread and fasten off. Resist the temptation to draw up the stitches too tightly. There has to be enough slack to allow the elastic to slide. Adjust the elastic as needed; sew the overlapped ends securely through both thicknesses.

No-Sew Elastic Option

If your skirt is not too heavy for a super-lightweight sort of elastic, or if you prefer a more pliable waistline, you can insert rounds of narrow elastic through the backs of the crochet stitches. Crochet a five-round single crochet waistband the same way as the solid elastic casing option above. Cut three lengths of narrow braided or round elastic to fit around your waist, plus an inch or two. Thread one elastic onto a blunt needle. On the inside of the waistband, stitch through the backs of the stems of the sc of Rnd 1, drawing the elastic evenly through the round as you go. Temporarily secure the ends of the elastic. Repeat with the next elastic, going through the backs of Rnd 3, repeat with the next elastic, going through the backs of Rnd 5. Adjust the elastics to fit and sew or knot the ends together.

RESOURCES

STITCHES AND SYMBOLS

Foundation Single Crochet (fsc)

I am an enthusiastic supporter of this technique. No more too-tight base chains that choke up or too-loose ones that sag. This method creates a foundation chain and row of sc at the same time, easy, sturdy and elastic—quite an elegant solution, especially useful for necklines and waistlines.

FSC AS A FLAT FOUNDATION:

First Stitch   Ch 2, insert hook into the 2nd ch from hook (into the front face of the chain and under the nub at the back of the chain) under 2 loops (a), YO and draw up a loop (b) (2 loops on hook); YO and draw through 2 loops on hook (c).

Second Stitch   Insert hook under 2 strands at the forward edge of the stem of the previous sc (d). It will resemble the way you insert the hook into a chain. YO and draw up a loop (2 loops on hook); YO and draw through one loop on hook. You have just made the "chain" that lies along the base of the foundation (2 loops on hook); YO and draw through 2 loops on hook (e). You have just made the "sc".

Third Stitch   Insert hook into the "chain" at the base of the stitch just made, into the front face and under the back nub, under 2 strands (f), YO and draw up a loop (2 loops on hook); YO and draw through one loop on hook. You have just made the chain. YO and draw through 2 loops on hook (g). You have just made the sc.
Repeat the 3rd stitch across, except at the end.

Last Stitch   Insert hook into the "chain," under 2 strands. YO and draw up a loop, YO and draw through 2 loops on hook (h).
Note: Notice that the first and last Fsc stitches are missing a step and thus are a bit shorter than the others. I like to compress the ends of this foundation. It keeps the ends neater when you work your first row of stitches.

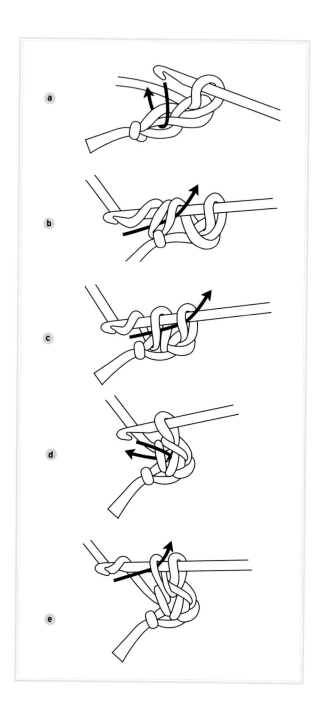

The Fsc is also useful for adding stitches at the end of a row or when joining the underarm of a seamless garment. You can make a Fsc after completing any stitch. The stitch just made before the Fsc will always have two loops at the top of the stitch, the ones you would normally work under. Just below that, there are strands that form the "stem." Whatever the stitch, you will begin the Fsc by inserting the hook under two strands of the forward edge of the stem of the stitch just made, closest to the top loops of the stitch. I always call for a ch 1 to begin, so as not to compress the end. Skip the First Stitch above, work the Second Stitch, then make Fsc as needed.

Esc (extended single crochet) Insert hook in the next st, YO and draw up a loop (2 loops on hook); YO and draw through one loop on hook, YO and draw through 2 loops on hook.

Rev sc (reverse single crochet) Moving in the reverse direction, from left to right, insert hook in the next st, make sc.

Trtr (treble triple crochet) YO 4 times, insert hook in next st, YO and draw up a loop (6 loops on hook), [YO and draw through 2 loops on hook] 5 times.

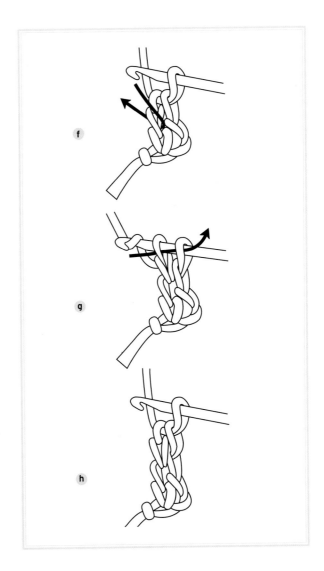

Stitch Key

Abbreviations for special techniques, stitches, or stitch combinations are explained in the box at the beginning of each pattern, among them Tss, Cl, Sh, V, and Bob. Here is a list of common abbreviations I've used throughout:

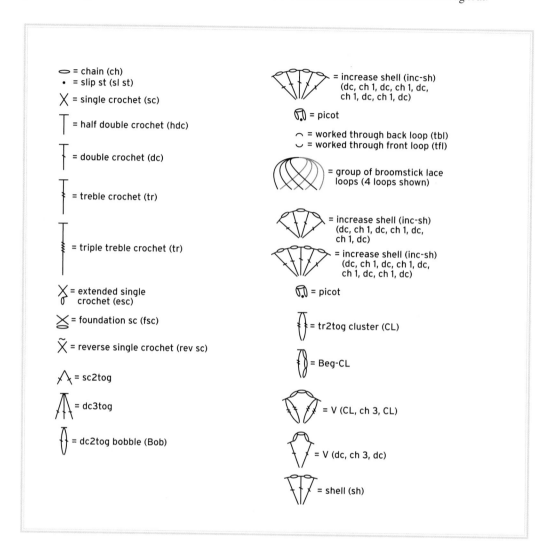

Abbreviations

ch chain, chain stitch

ch- refers to a chain or space previously made

ch-sp chain space

Cl cluster

dc double crochet

dc2tog double crochet two stitches together

dtr double triple crochet

hdc half double crochet

lp(s) loop, loops

patt pattern, patterns

rnd(s) round, rounds

RS right side

sc single crochet

sc2tog single crochet two together

sl st slip stitch

sp space

st stitch

tch turning chain

tbl through the back loop

tfl through the front loop

tog together

tr triple or treble crochet

WS wrong side

YO yarn over

Yarn Substitution Chart

Ball band symbols for yarn weight are the standardized system created by the Craft Yarn Council of America. See and download a complete handbook of Yarn Standards and Guidelines from the CYCA sponsored Web site, www.yarnstandards.com.

YARN WEIGHT SYMBOL & CATEGORY NAMES	0 LACE	1 SUPER FINE	2 FINE	3 LIGHT	4 MEDIUM	5 BULKY	6 SUPER BULKY
Type of Yarns in Category	Fingering 10-count crochet thread	Sock, Fingering, Baby	Sport, Baby	DK, Light Worsted	Worsted, Afghan, Aran	Chunky, Craft, Rug	Bulky, Roving
Crochet Gauge* Ranges in Single Crochet to 4 in.	32–42 double crochets**	21–32 sts	16–20 sts	12–17 sts	11–14 sts	8–11 sts	5–9 sts
Recommended Hook in Metric Size Range	Steel*** 1.6–1.4 mm	2.25–3.5 mm	3.5–4.5 mm	4.5–5.5 mm	5.5–6.5 mm	6.5–9 mm	9 mm and larger

Guidelines Only: The above reflect the most commonly used gauges and needle or hook sizes for specific yarn categories.

** Lace-weight yarns are usually knitted or crocheted on larger needles and hooks to create lacy, openwork patterns. Accordingly, a gauge range is difficult to determine. Always follow the gauge stated in your pattern.

*** Steel crochet hooks are sized differently from regular hooks—the higher the number, the smaller the hook, which is the reverse of regular hook sizing. (Source: Craft Yarn Council of America, www.YarnStandards.com)

Conversion Chart

U.S. TERM	U.K./AUS TERM
dc double crochet	tr treble crochet
hdc half double crochet	htr half treble crochet
sc single crochet	dc double crochet
sl st slip stitch	sc single crochet
tr treble crochet	dtr double treble crochet

YARNS

If the yarns featured in this book are not available at your local shop, contact the yarn companies below or visit the Web sites for stores and/or ordering info.

Artyarns
39 Westmoreland Avenue
White Plains, New York 10606
914-428-0333
www.artyarns.com

**Caron International/
NaturallyCaron.com**
Customer Service
P. O. Box 222
Washington, NC 27889
1-800-868-9194
www.caron.com
www.naturallycaron.com

Coats & Clark/Red Heart/Moda Dea Consumer Services
P. O. Box 12229
Greenville, SC 29612-0229
800-648-1479
www.coatsandclark.com

**Fairmount Fibers/
Manos del Uruguay Yarns**
915 North 28th Street
Philadelphia, PA 19130
888-566-9970
info@fairmountfibers.com
www.fairmountfibers.com

Feza Yarns
453 Pepper Street
Monroe, CT 06468
203-261-3982
www.fezayarns.com

Lanaknits Designs/Hemp For Knitting
Suite 3B
320 Vernon Street, Nelson, BC V1L4E4
Canada
1-888-301-0011
info@lanaknits.com
www.hempforknitting.com

Plymouth Yarn Company, Inc
500 Lafayette Street
Bristol, PA 19007
215-788-0459
pyc@plymouthyarn.com
www.plymouthyarn.com

South West Trading Company
918 South Park Lane, Suite 102
Tempe, AZ 85281
866- 794-1818
info@soysilk.com
www.soysilk.com

**Tahki Stacy Charles, Inc./
Filatura Di Crosa**
70-30 80th Street, Building #36
Ridgewood, NY 11385
800-338-YARN
www.tahkistacycharles.com

TOOLS

All the crochet tools, accessories, beading supplies, and sewing notions used in the production of this book are available at major craft stores and online.

Annie's Attic
www.anniesattic.com

Jo-Ann Fabric and Craft Stores
www.joann.com

Michaels Stores, Inc.
www.michaels.com

I've played with the following reasonably priced Tunisian tools and highly approve:

• ChiaoGoo Bamboo Tunisian hooks, 9" and 13" lengths, from size E-4 (3.5mm) through P (11.5mm) and ChiaoGoo Bamboo Flexible Cable hooks. Visit www.chiaogoo.com for product information, or order at www.bargainyarns.com
• The new Denise Interchangeable Crochet Hooks are here and are completely interchangeable with the Denise knitting needle cables. You can make whatever size or length flexible cable crochet hook you need, perfect for big gauge or wide row Tunisian applications.
Visit www.knitdenise.com for product and ordering information."

FOR FURTHER INSTRUCTION

For information and instruction on crocheting, knitting, and more, visit the Craft Yarn Council of America Web site.
www.craftyarncouncil.com

Join the Crochet Guild of America, come to the conferences, and take the classes. I did!
www.crochet.org

See video tutorials for Broomstick, Hairpin, and Tunisian, find specialty tools and a lot of other majorly cool stuff at Jennifer Hansen's site. She does the techniques differently than I do, but she's amazing.

Stitch Diva Studios
www.stitchdiva.com

CROCHET SPOKEN HERE

Check out these sites to commune with like-minded crocheters and other fiberazzi.

Crochetville
www.crochetville.org

CrochetMe
www.crochetme.com

Crochet Soirée
www.crochetsoiree.com

My blog
www.doriseverydaycrochet.blogspot.com

Ravelry
www.ravelry.com

FOR FURTHER READING

Books

Crochet Patterns Book 300. Nihon Vogue, 2006.

The current darlings among my crochet buds are stitch guides in Japanese, so you'll have to rely on the stitch symbol diagrams to use them. They are way expensive and hard-to-get, but worth every yen. Search for Japanese publishers like Nihon Vogue and Ondori. I especially like this one from Nihon Vogue.

Grabowski, Angela "ARNie." *Encyclopedia of Tunisian Crochet. Abilene*, TX: LoneStar Abilene Publishing, LLC, 2004.

If you're gonna be serious about Tunisian, you will want this self-published work, considered by many Tunisian freaks as the guide. Visit www.chezcrochet.com to order.

Knight, Erika, ed. *The Harmony Guides*, Basic Crochet Stitches. Loveland, CO: Interweave Press, 2008.

A new, spruced-up edition of a favorite stitch guide.

Manthey, Karen, and Susan Brittain. *Crocheting for Dummies*. Hoboken, NJ: Wiley Publishing Inc., 2004.

For general reference.

Thompson, Pamela. *Hairpin Crochet Technique and Design*. London, UK: B.T. Batsford, Ltd., 1983.

A hard-to-find volume today, this is an interesting and informative guide to where Hairpin crochet has been.

Waldrep, Mary Carolyn, ed. *Big Book of Favorite Crochet Patterns*. Dover Needlework Series. Mineola, New York: Dover Publications, 1991.
—*The Crocheter's Treasure Chest*. Dover Needlework Series. Mineola, New York: Dover Publications, 1989.
—*Floral Crochet*. Dover Needlework Series. Mineola, New York: Dover Publications, 1987.
—*150 Favorite Crochet Designs*. Dover Needlework Series. Mineola, NY: Dover Publications, 1995.

For the ultimate inspiration, this series of books is still in print, featuring vintage thread patterns with lace that I can't stop drooling over.

Magazines

Find More of my work in these publications

Crochet!
www.crochetmagazine.com

Crochet Today
www.crochettoday.com

Interweave Crochet
www.interweavecrochet.com

Acknowledgments

Hey, Mom, Harry, and Nick! I thank my family for their support, even though they can't understand why I would do this again.

One normally does not need to thank the better half of one's brain. In this case I really do, for without Karen Manthey—her brilliant illustrations and technical advice—this would be but half a book. Karen, you rock!

To the team at Potter Craft, editors and staff, present and past, including but not limited to: editors Betty Wong, Erica Smith, Jennifer Graham, Melissa Bonventre, publicist Ava Kavyani, Art Director Chi Ling Moy and Designer La Tricia Watford, and to queen bees Victoria Craven, Rosy Ngo, Jenny Frost, and Lauren Shakely, I offer my gratitude and one parting line:"Sorry about the mess!"

I now have an adorable author photo thanks to Heather Weston, who fell in love with my gray hair and insisted on shooting me. I'll take it!

Brava to the drop-dead gorgeous models who smiled and twirled their way through countless costume changes. Thanks for making my stuff look so good.

I appreciate the Musketeers, including Diane Moyer, Vashti Braha and Tammy Hildebrand, plus my buds Teresa Lawson, Susie Malone, and Suzanne Halstead for knowing when to say something nice and most of all for knowing when not to call, write, or otherwise halt the train of thought.

For yarn shipments and support above and beyond, I thank fiber benefactors and staff, present and past: Stacy Charles and Debbie Skinner at Tahki Stacy Charles, Cari Clement and Liz Walsh at Caron International, Terri Geck at Coats&Clark, Lisa Myers at Fairmount Fibers, Jonelle Raffino and Kat Cade at South West Trading Company, JoAnne Turcotte at Plymouth Yarns, Lana Hames and Laurel Smith at Lanaknits; Ivy Strausberg at DMC; and Chava and Emir at Feza.

For your inspiration and nagging, I thank all the wonderful crocheters I've met, in person and online. You have taught me more than I can express.

Thanks to the coffee bean–producing areas of the planet for the heavenly, stimulating brew without which this book would not have been thinkable.

And thanks to my pack, John and alpha-Chihuahua Cookie. I enjoyed the change-up in the take-out foods this time around, including the occasional double-whopper-with-cheese-no-onion.

INDEX

Published in the United States by Potter Craft,
an imprint of the Crown Publishing Group, a
division of Random House, Inc., New York.

www.crownpublishing.com
www.pottercraft.com

POTTER CRAFT and colophon is a registered
trademark of Random House, Inc.

Library of Congress
Cataloging-in-Publication Data

Chan, Doris.

Crochet lace innovations : 20 dazzling designs in
broomstick, hairpin, tunisian, and exploded lace /
Doris Chan.
    p. cm.
  ISBN 978-0-307-46382-1
  1. Crocheting--Patterns. 2. Lace and lace making-
-Patterns. I. Title.
  TT820.C426 2010
  746.2'2--dc22
                            2009027689

Printed in China

Design by La Tricia Watford
Photography by Heather Weston

10 9 8 7 6 5 4 3

First Edition